THE MADNESS OF MOSCOW

*One man's journey of
life and love in Russia*

CARY JOHNSTON

Matador
9 Priory Business Park,
Wistow Road, Kibworth Beauchamp,
Leicestershire. LE8 0RX
Tel: 0116 279 2299
Email: books@troubador.co.uk
Web: www.troubador.co.uk/matador
Twitter: @matadorbooks

ISBN 978 1789015 591

British Library Cataloguing in Publication Data.
A catalogue record for this book is available from the British Library.

Printed and bound in Great Britain by 4edge Limited
Typeset in 11pt Minion Pro by Troubador Publishing Ltd, Leicester, UK

Matador is an imprint of Troubador Publishing Ltd

'Your elbow is close, yet you can't bite it'

Russian proverb

CONTENTS

FOREWORD

BY FRED DINENAGE

*(Official biographer to the bestselling
Kray twins book* Our Story)

Timing, they say, is everything. So, as I write – with the international row over the nerve agent attack in the UK city of Salisbury still ongoing, and the alleged involvement of the Russians – the timing of this book could hardly have been better. And what a book it is! This is the story of one man's experiences in Moscow, presenting programmes for Russia Today, a TV station with a news agenda giving the Russian view of world affairs. Cary talked his way into the job – and clinched it by telling the only joke he knew! – and found himself in midwinter Moscow, without a clue of what was ahead of him – and without understanding more than half a dozen words of Russian.

This is the fascinating tale of his experiences… His search for the perfect Russian bride… His involvement with various ladies along the way… His escape from fascist thugs… And his face-to-face encounter with one Vladimir Putin.

'I nodded my head at him and he flicked his head upwards in reply, as if to say: Yes, I've acknowledged your existence, and that's more than enough for you.'

Cary's journey reminded me so much of my only visit to Moscow – then in very much a communist Russia – for the 1980 Olympic Games. An event clouded by controversy and boycotted by the Americans and several other countries, because of the Soviet Union's invasion of Afghanistan. The UK didn't boycott the Games, but Prime Minister Margaret Thatcher made it clear she would have preferred the BBC and ITV not to have been there.

We were all summoned to a briefing at the Foreign Office and told the British Embassy in Moscow would be closed for the duration of the Games – and also warned: 'You are on your own if any of you get into any trouble.' The atmosphere was intimidating and claustrophobic and we were under surveillance – as indeed were Cary and his colleagues. He tells us that there's a spy, an informer, in every office. But Cary's journalistic experience – he is a quality TV reporter and presenter – saw him through it all. Not to mention a fair degree of charm!

Nonetheless, for him this was a real baptism of fire. It's a revealing insight into life in Russia. And, it has to be said, a revealing insight into one Cary Johnston. I thoroughly enjoyed this book. As the Russians might say: 'Intriguyushchiy.'

Intriguing!

PROLOGUE

What on earth goes on in the heads of Russians? On the one hand they seem content to live under the feet of any pseudo-dictatorship (communist, Soviet, Mafia or otherwise) while on the other hand they want to throw off the chains of their dreadful past and enjoy all the trappings of a flashy Western lifestyle. You can't have both, yet for some reason they seem unable to comprehend the paradox.

The people of any nation are formed and indeed often scarred by their history and whatever upheavals they have endured, and certainly the story of Russia and the wider Soviet Union has been traumatic to say the least. Stalin's death camps, the Second World War, the years of stagnation and corruption – you can see why they would be a bit fed up. Above all, they want to be respected for their abilities both culturally and economically, yet ask any Russian what kind of car they would like to buy, and not one of them will mention a Russian-made vehicle. They want Toyotas, Peugeots, or (if they are loaded) Mercedes and BMWs. A Russian-made Lada? Not on your life. They are deeply suspicious of the military intentions of NATO and the political manoeuvrings of the United States, yet give any Russian a choice of where to live and they will come back with a list of Western destinations as long as your arm. Paris or Siberia? London or Vladivostok? New York or Moscow? For Russians, it's a no-brainer – the Western destination wins every time.

And so it was into this cauldron of contradictions that I threw myself head-first, hoping to gain a first-hand insight into what motivates this seemingly strange nation, what the Russian people want out of their present lives and what they hope for in the future. For years it's been a largely misunderstood place, which when you think about it, is scandalous and terrifying. After all, how can we be so ignorant of a nation that is the largest in the world? Indeed, even that single fact is often lost on many of us. Ask your friends to name the biggest country on our planet by land mass, and see how many reply 'America' or 'China' or 'Australia'. You'll be surprised.

I was also hoping to discover if the cultural clichés about Russians were true. I mean, a Russian man without vodka is like politics without sleaze – it can't happen, right? And Russian women are all queuing up at registry offices to marry the first gullible socially inadequate Western man that comes along, right? And, if I'm being honest, I was indeed hoping to find the Russian girl of my dreams, to fulfil my genuinely held yearning for a lifelong partner, which had thus far eluded me in the West. But would the dream tally with reality?

Here then, is my experience of living in modern-day Moscow. Warts and all. And like everything else in life, the truth is often stranger (if not *weirder*) than fiction. It is a personal insight into life in a very alien land. I'm no cultural historian. Nor am I a foreign correspondent. But I know a good tale when I see one and Russia is full of stories, characters and surprises. If you only raise one eyebrow at the following true events, then I would already have made a difference. If you raise two, then my job is done.

1

NATASHA

'Beautiful, charming, intriguing
and all the other Russian girl clichés'

Going out with a Russian girl is like going to see a magic show – you know you're being tricked, you just can't work out how. Imagine – the magician is on stage with a big black cloth bag in his hand. He opens it up and puts in a hapless white rabbit. Then he looks at you and asks, 'Where's the rabbit?' And you reply, 'It's in the bag.' Then he invites you to have a look, and – Hey Presto! – the rabbit is *not* in the bag. And you wonder, 'How did that happen?'

Well, that's what it's like with a Russian girl. The moment you think the relationship is 'in the bag' you can guarantee it isn't. That's not when your work finishes, that's when your work begins. I know this, because of

Natasha. Now Natasha appeared to be anything *but* your typical Russian girl. We met at one of those business and social networking events that tries very hard to pretend it's more than just a dating cattle market, and given that I was indeed on the lookout for a long-term partner, I could hardly complain. This one came complete with a website promising a meeting place of 'global minds' and worldly-wise exciting professionals. In fairness, many of the events they had planned were rather good. Restaurants, theatre outings, trips to the cinema and poetry readings (if you like that kind of thing). So with an open mind, I went along to one of their dinner parties. It was being held in a huge Georgian-style restaurant in the centre of Moscow. On arrival, someone ticked off my name on the list, before I wandered into the private area they had booked, whilst trying to look relaxed, though feeling distinctly nervous. I was confronted by a long wooden table with around twenty people already seated. First thing – don't get stuck in a corner with a load of blokes; that would defeat the object of coming in the first place, wouldn't it? Though actually, I need not have worried, as the ratio between women and men was about four to one. I sat strategically near the end where there were already four women – beautiful, charming, intriguing and all the other Russian girl clichés right here in front of me. And there she was. Slim, dark-haired, green-eyed and elegantly dressed in a black skirt and crisp white formal shirt, with silver cufflinks – giving off a distinct air of 'I am an intelligent businesswoman not to be messed with, but if you play your cards right, you might get something else too.' She flicked a look at me.

'Hello, I'm Cary,' I said assertively, doing my best alpha male impression.

'I'm Natasha,' she replied, with a guarded smile and steady gaze.

This, I ventured, even after just one look, was definitely on the cards. Sometimes you can just tell. The electricity was already crackling between us, without even the need for the customary alcoholic drink to loosen our inhibitions.

So what happened with Natasha? Well, I shall get to that eventually. But actually, I am somewhat ahead of myself. About a year ahead. You may be wondering what I was doing in Moscow in the first place. And indeed, querying my statement that Natasha was not a 'typical Russian girl'. What then *is* a typical Russian girl? Let me take you on my journey…

It was January. I had just landed in the middle of the night at Moscow international airport and a brief look out of the aeroplane window revealed what I had always suspected. A metre of snow and ice on the ground, blizzard-like conditions and a temperature of minus twenty-five, or at least that's what the captain had just said. I was surprised the plane hadn't just skidded off the runway; a runway that was being cleared of snow by an army of burly sour-looking Russians with shovels in their great bear-like hands – some weren't even wearing gloves. As I looked around the cabin at the ugly rough-cut Russian blokes and their stunning much taller blonde-haired girlfriends, every story I had ever heard about Russia seemed to have been confirmed. All I needed to complete the picture was a few vodka-fuelled drunks, some brown bears running around on the tarmac, a couple of sexy James Bond-style female spies, and some people wearing funny fur hats.

'Ladies and gentlemen, we have arrived at Moscow Sheremetyevo airport. Thank you for flying with Aeroflot,' crackled the captain's Russian-accented voice.

And so began my adventure into a country of which I knew very little about. To be fair, I had studied the politics of the Soviet Union and Eastern Europe in my student days. So as far as general knowledge was concerned, I knew that the last Tsar of Russia was called Nicholas the Second, though curiously the one before that was not Nicholas the First. I never found out why. I did not speak Russian, and what culture I thought I knew was mostly gleaned from films starring the aforementioned James Bond – hardly an education, though I remember that *The Spy Who Loved Me* with Roger Moore (the best Bond) was a good one, and that definitely had a sexy Russian female spy in it.

So really, a complete leap into the dark. And as I took my first steps onto Russian soil – well, the snow-covered tarmac – in the biting wind and swirling snow, I asked myself, 'Why would anyone live in a place like this? For that matter, why did anyone even build a city here? What the hell were they thinking? And what am I doing here?' That last question, I could answer.

In brief, I had spent ten years as a news reporter at the BBC in London, then ten years as a journalist at a regional ITV channel, before moving to Spain for some sunshine and adventure. I had four happy years living by the coast of Andalusia, before reality spoiled the party in the form of the world financial crisis. I no longer had any work – and no amount of sun, sea and sangria was going to make up for the fact that I couldn't pay the mortgage. Realising the seriousness of the situation, I started trawling job websites like any other unemployed person. Funny, that word 'unemployed'. In conversations, people ask you, 'So what do you do?' And never do you reply, 'I'm unemployed.' Somehow it's like saying, 'I am a total failure and a social outcast.' So instead we all say, 'I'm between jobs.' Yeah, right.

So there I was, miserable and unemployed, sitting around with nothing to do except worry about the future. And at the end of another unrewarding morning of job-searching on the internet, I closed my laptop and began randomly flicking through TV channels, marvelling at how much rubbish was on. It was then that I came across an English-speaking news channel sandwiched somewhere between BBC News and Al Jazeera. The logo in the corner said RT. 'What's that?' I wondered. Further viewing revealed it stood for 'Russia Today' and was broadcasting from Moscow, with a news agenda giving a Russian world view of things. And suddenly it dawned on me. I knew how to present news and I was interested in Russia, what with my university background and all. It's an obvious fit – ring them! Several phone calls, emails and general haranguing of switchboard operators and secretaries, finally led to the chance of an interview in London with the then news director at the channel. I ran for the airport. Little did I know that the following few months would change my life forever.

The interview was to take place in the lobby area of a hotel in Piccadilly. I was suited-up, tie straight, rehearsing all my answers, when this guy arrived wearing just a pair of jeans and a polo shirt. This immediately unbalanced me slightly, as I felt rather overdressed. Was his casual attire deliberate? I also realised it was to be my first meeting with a 'real' Russian. A thickset middle-aged man called Alexey, with a precise close-cut designer beard and a manner which I was struggling to work out, veering from friendly and colloquial to piercingly intellectual. Quietly spoken, yet with a tone that betrayed a certain steeliness. And then, he put me to the sword.

'Name all the countries that were associated with the former Soviet Union,' he said with deadly calmness.

'Er...' I stammered.

'What year was the Berlin Wall erected?' he continued.

'Er...'

'Who was the penultimate Tsar of Russia?' came the next shot.

'Er...'

This unrelenting KGB-style interrogation nightmare continued for what seemed ages, before yet another unbalancing question was thrust in my direction. Well, less of a question and more of a demand.

'Tell me a joke,' he said.

'Pardon?' I replied bewildered.

'We are interested in well-rounded people who can fit in with a social group. Tell me a joke.'

Given that I was not a natural joke-teller or stand-up comedian (I am no Michael McIntyre or Bill Bailey) and deciding to err on the side of safety and not relate anything blue, I went for the only joke I knew in the whole wide world.

'A man goes to the doctor and says, "Doctor, doctor, I think I'm turning into a pig." So the doctor asks, "How long has this been going on for?" And the man replies, "Aweeeeeeeek."'

It worked. My joke had elicited a smile, the first of the interview and at that moment I thought to myself, 'Maybe this job could actually be mine.'

Two weeks later, it was.

I had accepted a role as a news presenter on a one-year rolling contract. Enough time to live and work in a strange country. To explore a nation and its people. To sort out my flailing love life. Everyone I spoke to thought I was mad. In fact, every single conversation with every single friend I had, went the same way.

'I'm going to live and work in Moscow.'

'Moscow!'

'Yes, Moscow.'

'What, with all that snow and the Gulag?'

'Well, I'm not sure I'll be sent to the Gulag, but...'

'Are you crazy?'

So friends aside, finally there I was queuing up at the Russian passport control area at Moscow airport, waiting to get my document stamped. First rule of Russia – there's a lot of waiting to be done. I looked around the bare hall. There were about five hundred people crammed into several different lines. I say 'lines' but they were really just hordes of people all jostling each other in a bid to get to one of the five passport officer booths that were open, as several different planes had arrived at more or less the same time, leading to an enormous logjam. I had never seen anything like it. The Russian passport officers themselves were in no hurry. A good long surly look at your face, a good long scan of your passport, another good long surly look at your face, followed by a good long nothing in particular, with a stare that said, 'I'm suspicious of you.' Trouble was, all of a sudden two of the officers decided it was time for a break and simply closed their booths. Just like that. Leaving two scrums of people no choice but to try and hijack the other queues. Arguments broke out as Russians remonstrated with each other, whilst bemused foreigners stood around with their wheelie bags wondering what on earth was going on.

'*Ya zhdal dvatsat minoot!*' bellowed a burly Russian guy, complaining about how long he'd been waiting.

'*Oo minya balit galava!*' complained an old lady, explaining how the situation was giving her a headache. And me? Well, I was just letting it all sink in and wash over me. When you're on an adventure in a foreign land, even difficult moments can be somehow fascinating and you need to have patience. Waving your arms around and shouting, 'I'm British! Let me through!' does not wash with passport control officials. At the booth, the officer stared at me again, with a look of granite. Then he started flicking through the pages of my passport. Then another look at me and another look down. This could go on all day, I thought. And then... from his pocket he fished out a miniature magnifying glass, I kid you not, and started squinting through it at each and every page of my passport. By now, the people behind me had given up and moved on to a different throng, thinking that the examination of my documents was going to take an age. They were right. It did. But I kept my nerve and remained silent and unmoving throughout. Eventually he relented, by begrudgingly stamping my passport and pressing the button to release the glass doors. I was through. I then collected my bags and with stunning naivety simply walked outside into the snowy night with nothing more than a pair of thin trousers and a light jacket. That's when it hit me. A cold that took my breath away. I had experienced below zero temperatures in Britain before of course, say around minus five or so, but minus *twenty*-five is another ball game. You then realise that you have about ten minutes to find shelter before your eyes turn into little round ice balls and your feet and hands go numb. Mental check to get some proper Russian winter gear. The stuff I was wearing was useless.

A taxi driver had been booked for me. His name was Anton. A tall, well-built jovial fellow, with blue eyes, a mop of brown hair, and a keen interest in anything outside Russia. He had never been abroad and was fascinated by foreign lands. Every two minutes he came out with a question in broken English.

'Cary, how much cost petrol in England?'

'Cary, what you do in Spain?'

'Cary, why you come Soviet Union?'

'Cary, what you think of Russian girls?'

Ah, now *there* was a question that aroused my interest.

'Well, they seem very beautiful in TV shows and in fashion magazines,' I said cautiously. He smiled.

'Maybe you marry Russian girl, yes?'

'Maybe,' I replied, wondering where this conversation was going, but too tired from the flight to explore it further, though my gut feeling told me that Russian women were going to feature heavily in my time here.

For now though, the journey to the hotel where I would be staying for a few days was about an hour's drive away. My new employer would be paying for it and I would use my time there to find some proper rented accommodation. Also, it meant I had a few days to sort myself out, before I was actually due to start work at the TV station. It seemed a good plan. I fended off my fatigue and looked curiously out of the window of the car I was being driven in. The scenery passing by was nothing to speak of, just the normal kind of concrete industrial areas you'd expect to see in the suburbs of any city really, though there did seem to be an inordinate amount of pollution in the air, with a heavy throat-clogging haze that was already beginning to irritate my larynx, despite the fact that I had barely spent more than five minutes in the open. The vents in Anton's car were blasting out warm air, as the squeaky and inadequate wipers struggled to push away the torrents of snow that were belting down onto the windscreen – a windscreen that had a large jagged crack from one side to the other. I imagined that driving a car in that condition anywhere in Western Europe would have been dangerous if not illegal, but out here cracks in the glass didn't seem to matter, and Anton appeared completely unconcerned.

'What happened to your windscreen?' I ventured.

He gave no answer, but simply shrugged, while huge filthy lorries thundered past us, throwing up waves of icy slush and sludge onto the windscreen. Every vehicle was covered in grey-brown dirt – you couldn't even read the number plates. Eventually we arrived at the hotel, situated somewhere on the edge of town, and Anton dropped me off with my bags and said goodbye, leaving me his number in case I needed a taxi in the future.

The hotel lobby was drab green and grey, a dark and dingy place that looked like nothing had changed since 1950, and when I approached the reception desk, it was clear that no English was spoken here. A lot of sign language and smiling on my part eventually stirred the elderly, miserable-looking receptionist into some kind of action. Unwillingly, she wrenched a huge decrepit old book from its perch on a big wooden shelf and slammed it down on the desk, throwing up a pile of dust. Hundreds of handwritten pages, most yellow with age, were flipped over by her weary hand, until a free page was found. She scribbled something down and stamped the book in three places, before thrusting the keys to my room into my hands. Not a word was spoken. The lifts were in the corner, so I dragged my bags towards them, realising at once how hungry I was. The room itself was tiny, with a bed as soft as a blancmange and bedsprings that squealed in unison like some kind of mousey chorus. A stained green carpet, brown peeling wallpaper, a rickety old wardrobe, and a falling-to-bits bedside table completed the dismal picture. A pocket-sized TV was perched on the table and I turned it on. A fuzzy old Soviet film was in progress, with the actors naturally enough speaking in Russian. There were a few other channels, but nothing in English. There was, however, a tiny shower unit in the bathroom, with hot water, and a tiny shard of soap. Sometimes you just have to appreciate the simple things in life, and the hot shower after my long journey did indeed feel like luxury, as the sounds of the Russian TV drama wafted into the bathroom, reminding me that I was really here, in a foreign place, where people spoke a foreign language and no one seemed to smile. And I was ravenous. I got dressed and went back to the reception area, cannily picking up a combined Moscow street map and Metro plan, which had been discarded on a table.

'Where is the dining room please?' I asked hopefully. Blank faces were turned in my direction. It turned out that the dining room was really an extension of the bar, but there was no food being prepared because it was too late; the chefs had all gone home. And there were no nuts or crisps at the bar either. I looked at my watch – 9.30pm. What to do? Well, in most capital cities you would just go out, find the nearest restaurant and pig out, right? But here on the edge of town in Moscow, I discovered it was not that easy.

With much finger-pointing, I was directed to a basement eatery three blocks down the street. I had a few thousand euros of savings in my pocket, all my worldly money which I had brought with me to last for a while until I got paid. It may seem like a lot of cash to be carrying around, but I didn't as yet have a Russian bank account, so couldn't transfer any money into the country, and who knew how much rent and living expenses I would need up front in the meantime. Would I need to buy a car, for example? I had also heard that Russians didn't much like credit cards, and that traveller's cheques were largely frowned upon. In any case, I had intended to change it into roubles on arrival at the airport, but in all the kerfuffle at the passport queue, I had forgotten. So, here was the dilemma. Do I leave the money in a strange, insecure-looking hotel room, or do I take it with me and hope I don't get mugged? I decided on the latter, so with a deep breath I ventured out into the unfamiliar, dark, snow-covered streets. It was exactly like any cliché I had ever seen about Moscow. Shuffling people wrapped in winter coats wearing big furry hats. The streets were grey and miserable and the concrete buildings uniformly ugly, stark and square. No variation between them. This was real Soviet construction of the kind I had always read about – quick, efficient and with something for everyone as long as it all looked the same, and as long as it all looked horrid. With my thin clothes offering little resistance to the biting cold and my feet already numb (I really would have to buy some proper fur-lined boots), I was happy to find the unpromising-looking basement bar in question and descended with some trepidation into its depths. I was greeted by the sight of a few long wooden benches, a bar at the far end and several Russians chatting and eating. It seemed lively enough and not too intimidating, despite the fact that I was the only foreigner, so my mood lightened somewhat. It was also warm. I sat down at one of the benches and a waitress eventually came over with a menu, which was all in Russian – a baffling language of odd back-to-front letters, which even Russians admit is a difficult system to master. But first, I thought I had better explain to the waitress that I didn't have any roubles.

'Do you accept euros?' I asked.

Blank faces again. Many shakes of heads later, it was clear they either didn't understand me, or they *did* understand me, but the answer to my question was, '*Nyet*' (No). Ah! I remembered I had a credit card! I fished it out of my pocket before waving it in the direction of the waitress, more in hope than anything. More shakes of heads. Credit cards were a relatively new phenomenon here, as were ATM machines (I hadn't seen any up to this point) and in small bars like this the only currency that counted was cold, hard cash. And in roubles too. The waitresses and their customers were all staring at me with a mixture of curiosity and bemusement. It had probably been a long time since a foreigner had frequented this haunt, if ever. I was starting to shake with hunger. I was at a loss. It's amazing how helpless you can feel in an alien landscape. It's as if you have to unlearn everything you know and start again from scratch. But suddenly, some hope.

'I help you,' said an elderly Russian man dressed in green Russian army uniform. He had a few badges of honour pinned to his chest, which I assumed meant he had been decorated for his achievements in the field of action. He had close-cropped tawny hair, a square jaw and a lined forehead. His eyes were keen and philosophical. And he spoke broken English.

'Yes, please,' I replied, with an air of desperation.

'What is problem?'

'Well, I have no roubles, just euros.'

'Come with me.'

It's at that point that you have to rely on instinct. Carrying all that cash on the plane had seemed the sensible thing to do at the time. Now though, I felt very vulnerable.

I followed him outside into the snow. Where were we going? And more importantly, why was I following him? I put my fate into the hands of my gut feeling, and that feeling had decided that for some reason traipsing after a complete stranger down a dark snow-filled alleyway in Moscow, with all my money clutched to my chest and no clue where we were headed, somehow seemed the right thing to do at the time. The army man, whose name I did not know, turned around for a moment and beckoned me forward.

'Don't scared,' he said. 'I help you.'

Eventually, we came upon a small row of rickety food stalls, selling unappetizing-looking pies and sausages. Sandwiched in between was a tiny plastic booth with a half-broken, intermittently flashing, yellow neon sign above it, illuminating some messily hand-drawn numbers in black. This, it turned out, was a somewhat unofficial foreign exchange outlet. It looked exceedingly dodgy to me. The person hidden inside the booth looked nothing like a reputable financial worker and I wondered if I was about to be scammed big time. I looked around at the dark, scary streets and again drew upon my instincts. My army man piped up again.

'I come to protect,' he said.

Ah, so that was the idea. He had come along in case I got mugged or conned. At least I hoped so.

I huddled myself as close to the booth as possible while retrieving my money from my jacket pocket, cold white breath streaming out of my mouth, before pushing some of the notes under the makeshift counter with my shaking, blood-starved hands. The seedy-looking fellow inside grabbed them with his dirty nail-bitten fingers and picked up an old calculator. Without a word he punched some numbers in and held it up for me to see. I nodded in agreement, not really knowing if the figures were right or wrong and he carefully counted out the roubles. A minute later I was following my military chaperone back to the bar, the all-important roubles burning a hole in my pocket. As we entered, there were smiles from the assembled staff. A problem had been overcome and their source of curiosity had taken his first steps into Russian society. I thanked my army man profusely and offered to buy him a drink, but he calmly waved away my offers and went back to where he had been sitting, without a word. I picked up the menu again and just pointed to the first thing my fingers came to. A few minutes later what looked like some kind of goulash arrived at my table and a tentative smile broke out on my face. These Russians weren't all as humourless and unfriendly as I had first thought. My army man had saved me, without even accepting any form of recompense. I would probably face many more moments of misunderstanding as I began my exploration into the Russian way of life. I gratefully started to shovel the warming goulash into my mouth.

I felt I had arrived.

My new employers had assigned a property agent to find me somewhere to live, as by this time I was gagging to get out of the dingy hotel. I mused over whether they had chosen the hell-hole accommodation, as some kind of test. 'If he can put up with that, then he can put up with anything Moscow has to throw at him,' they had probably reasoned. Anyway, the agent turned out to be a portly middle-aged Russian lady called Marina, always wrapped in a massive real fur coat, while sporting a larger-than-life persona.

'Oh, Cary, my dear!' she shrieked on meeting me, in an exaggeratedly loud high-pitched voice, tottering along in black high-heeled boots.

'We find you apartment, yes, we find something nice, yes, like that, we find you!'

Marina's clients were like children to her, to be watched over and cared for and saved from the evil clutches of Moscow's unscrupulous landlords, of which there were many. You would think that finding an apartment would be simple enough in a big city. But without an understanding of the language, you were like a tiny boat lost at sea. How could you look for an advert in the paper? How could you ring and talk to a landlord? How could you hope to understand the contract?

Then there was the problem of actually finding an apartment that you wanted to view. All street names were written (reasonably enough) in Russian, and with the addresses back to front. So written addresses began with the street and block number and ended with the apartment number. For example, Novy Arbat 27, Apartment 15. So I was grateful for Marina's help. She told me that Russian landlords liked having foreign tenants, because they felt that foreigners were more reliable when it came to paying the rent. Did this mean that they basically regarded themselves as an untrustworthy race? How could that be? Though of course they could charge foreigners more, as generally speaking, foreigners earned more than the average Russian.

'Come, come,' said Marina. 'We see nice place now.'

I followed her down a main street like a baby chick following a mother hen, with huge tenement style buildings towering above us on either side of what seemed to be a major highway into the centre of town. We were in an area called Frunzenskaya, considered to be a safe part of town and not far from my workplace. One thing I was learning about Moscow was that nothing was ever what it seemed from the outside. An imposing blank steel doorway could easily lead to a palatial restaurant or bar on the inside. There was no concept of proper marketing or advertising a business. As a result, many supermarkets, for example, were hidden from view inside a labyrinth of other unrelated services, with no signs or placards on the exterior to advise you of their existence within. Let's face it, in Soviet times there was no need for advertising was there? There was no private ownership and no chance of being an entrepreneur, so the idea of promoting a product was still a relatively new one for Russians – but more of the unexpected trials and tribulations of shopping a bit later. Back to the apartment search, it was clear that the steel front door syndrome also applied to accommodation, so when Marina opened the door to the block of the first apartment she wanted to show me, the entrance hall was pretty hideous. Rough concrete floors covered only by a muddy piece of cloth, all barely lit by a wall light which looked like it was about to fall out of its socket; dangerous-looking wires everywhere. Strewn all around were tin cans holding the discarded cigarette butts of committed smokers. For some reason, Russians found it acceptable to smoke in the corridors of apartment blocks, but not actually in their own apartments. The smell was grim. And this, *this*, was the centre of town. Not some poor outlying area, but a well-heeled hub of civilisation in the biggest country in the world. What a dump.

'No worry,' Marina reassured me, as she led me to the central lift apparatus. It was just like those old black and white films, where you have to wrench the iron gates apart to enter the lift, and you can see all the floors passing down as it clunks and shudders its way upwards. The apartment was on the top floor, which sounded good to me and indeed it turned out to be a perfectly acceptable pad, with wooden parquet flooring, a tiny kitchen, small balcony, and a few pieces of old Soviet furniture – a perfect place to base myself for now. I could always move somewhere better once I'd found my feet.

'I'll take it.'

The landlord was a Russian man in his fifties with a flat leather cap and beady eyes, who was happy enough to buy me a microwave and a new mattress for the bed. So with my stuff safely thrown on the floor and cash deposit handed over, I thanked Marina and headed out into the frosty morning air for my initial exploration of the area.

The first thing I noticed about the streets of Moscow was that they were not multi-cultural, at least not in the sense that I understood. As a person of colour (I have Jamaican heritage), I came to the conclusion that I was the only non-white person in town. I didn't come across any Indians or Arabs or South Americans or Chinese or Africans or any other race, creed or colour walking the streets, at least not initially. Just miserable pallid-looking Russians. And boy did I feel out of place. I suppose it would be the same for a white person walking through the streets of Lagos in Nigeria – for a while you are keenly aware of your colour and people's reactions to it. Did it matter? Well, firstly I had to change my mindset. There *were* different ethnicities, just none that I had seen before. Apart from the obvious Russians who were from this part of the country, there were also people from southern areas, known as the Caucasus, and also people from central Asian regions, darker-skinned folk with something (for want of a better phrase, so forgive me) Chinese-like about them. They seemed to be doing the less salubrious jobs, sweeping snow off the streets, packing shelves in supermarkets and driving unofficial taxis. As I continued walking, people would stare at me, then look away. Stare, then look away. I later discovered that they would stare not so much because I was black, but because I was simply not Russian. I could have been white, red, green or orange, and they would have stared just the same, but then looked away because whoever I was and whatever I was doing in Moscow, it was none of their business. A throwback to Soviet times I imagined, where people kept themselves to themselves, so as not to attract attention from the authorities. During the 1980 Olympic Games which were held in Moscow, the secret police would warn the public against talking to foreign athletes or journalists. It was a case of 'Why are you talking to that foreigner? Are you trying to defect?' And as much as the younger Russian generation may feel they have thrown off the shackles of those times, the brainwashing they received as kids from their parents still lingers in their subconscious. You can look, but don't get involved. Most of those who were staring at me probably assumed I was a diplomat, or at least working in one of the numerous foreign embassies here, and that would mean I was 'connected' so best to leave well alone.

I was to discover that the same applied to socialising. In Britain, if you invite a few friends over for dinner and drinks, then at some point in the future you could expect an invite back from your various guests. It's just the done thing. But in Russia it did not seem to happen with foreigners. If you invited a few people to your apartment – say Brits, Americans and Russians – only the Brits and Americans would invite you back. Why? Well, partly because of the secret police fear I explained earlier, and partly because the Russians felt embarrassed to invite you to their far more modest apartments. And by modest, I mean modest. Even Russians who had good jobs would be sharing a ramshackle room with shockingly run-down furniture and terrible fixtures and fittings, often with two other people. The women in particular faced this situation, as their wages were extraordinarily low compared to those of men. Often two women shared just one tiny room (beds, wardrobes, everything) and an even smaller kitchenette. How they managed to be so well turned out in such meagre circumstances would have me shaking my head in disbelief for months to come.

But as I always say, never be ashamed of where you live. Real friends come to see *you*, not your apartment. Nonetheless, Russians had clearly not got over this, assuming that Westerners would be shocked and upset. Nothing could be further from the truth, but I realised that getting beneath the skin of the society here would be harder than I had imagined. Also of course, my inability to speak the language did not help.

I continued walking until I came upon an entrance to one of Moscow's Metro stations. Hundreds of people were going in and out in the morning rush hour. Should I venture down? Yeah, why not! I unfolded the crumpled Metro map, which I'd picked up at the hotel and examined it carefully. I seemed to be at a station on the red line. The Metro was divided into different coloured lines and routes, much like any other Metro in the world I supposed. And with that in mind, I headed for the Metro entrance and was promptly pushed back by a throng of people exiting.

'*Nyet, nyet!*' they grunted at me, while physically shoving me back. It turned out that there was one set of doors for the entrance and a different set of doors for the exit, often around the corner. Blue stickers on the entrance doors, red on the exits. Okay, got it. I went around to the other side and entered into another world.

The sheer magnificence of the Moscow Metro takes your breath away. Huge domed ceilings, with mosaic pictures of Lenin showing the masses the way forward, or the Soviet hammer and sickle, all surrounded by real marble pillars, stained-glass facades or bronze statues. Massive and ornate chandeliers hanging down in rows, stretching down the length of each platform, with every bulb working, every piece of metalwork polished, and every Russian totally ignoring the magnificence all around them as they scurried around on their way to and from the office. An amazing work of art and beauty, ironically with much of the tunnelling done by forced labourers, under the orders of the dictator Stalin. I wondered how many people died in order to build it. Much the same as many other historic landmarks across the world. In the United States it's said that slave labour built the White House, yet we don't hear much about that, do we? And who the hell built Egypt's pyramids? I don't think they had JCBs in those days (and don't tell me it was aliens).

While I was pondering this, I noticed the metal ticket barriers and an old lady sitting in a Perspex-like booth next to them. I bought a ticket and clutching it I went up to the barrier wondering what to do. It turned out to be very simple. You just swiped your ticket over the front and it let you through. As I did this, a couple of young ticketless Russian hooligans vaulted the barriers and started running down the escalators. The lady in the booth leapt out and blew her whistle, though I didn't notice anyone running after them. At the same time, the barrier itself started playing a jaunty little five-second tune from little speakers, to alert the authorities that someone had gone through without paying. Each time someone went through illegally, this same little tune would ring out from the barrier. Later research revealed that the ditty was in fact the opening bars of a rather lovely classical composition by the eighteenth-century Polish composer Michal Kleofas Oginski called 'The Polonaise'. I wondered what he would have thought if he were alive today. All his lifetime of works condensed into a very un-orchestral five-second security alert on a load of ticket barriers on a Metro system. That would be the extent of his legacy. A bit like Pablo Picasso, whose name was used for an airport terminal in the city of Málaga in southern Spain. Imagine – one of the most innovative artists of the twentieth century, his name emblazoned across the departures hall of a big, square, ugly airport building. Not exactly the stuff of art. Still, better to be remembered in some form, than not at all I suppose. But why this composition was being used on the Moscow Metro, no one seemed to know. I soon learnt that if you asked a question about something quirky or odd in Russia, you would receive a stock answer, accompanied by a wry smile and a shrug of the shoulders.

'This is Russia,' they would say.

So with that in mind, I left Oginski's musical legacy behind and descended down the deep and steep escalator to the Metro platform. The trains operated like clockwork and I managed to get to Red Square without any trouble at all. It was the one place I wanted to see more than anywhere else. Throughout the years it's what I had seen on TV, with all those enormous Soviet military parades passing the podium of geriatric leaders as they presided over the hulking and creaking bulk of the former Soviet Union. Red Square is where Soviet troops marched on their way to do battle with the Nazis, eventually defeating Hitler's fascists. If you'd grown up in Britain like I had, you would assume that Winston Churchill alone had defeated Hitler, and if you had been raised in the United States, you would think that the U.S. Army had single-handedly saved the world, such is the plethora of cultural propaganda that we've been subjected to. The truth is it was a joint effort and the Soviets lost at least ten million soldiers fighting the German war machine, with maybe another ten million civilian casualties. In all, around a fifth of its population, a lot more proportionately than all the other Allies put together. Not that numbers alone can reflect suffering of course; it's just that the efforts of those from the former Soviet Union are often forgotten, in our consolidation of victory...

As the train neared the stop for Red Square, I stood up to exit. The door of the carriage swung open to reveal... a dead man lying on the platform. Right there in front of me. I knew he was a goner because he was just sprawled there unmoving on his back, with his neck in an odd position, arms akimbo, blood surrounding his partially bashed-in face. Jesus. Two policemen who looked like they'd spent too much time sitting in police cars eating burgers, were standing around the body, tilting up their oversized caps and scratching their heads. Meanwhile, rush hour commuters were literally stepping over the dead body in their zeal to get to work. Amazing. I mean, this was probably a murder scene. Surely they should be cordoning off the area and shutting down the station while they investigate? I was later to put this to a Russian colleague at my new workplace.

'Why didn't they close the Metro station? Vital evidence was probably being trodden on and lost with all those people walking over everything.'

'Shut the station?' she replied incredulously. 'Why should they shut the station? It was rush hour, are you mad?'

What an extraordinary reply. Was life that cheap here?

I walked carefully around the expanding pool of blood with a degree of horror, while others avoided it in the manner of people circumnavigating a puddle of water – a bit of a nuisance, but nothing to get too hot under the collar about.

So with my first dead body already under my belt (there would be another), I found myself on the edge of Red Square at last. I had to say that given the weight of history that the cobbled ground represented, it was rather incongruous to discover a whole load of market stalls selling trinkets to tourists, like plastic replica army badges, CCCP T-shirts, and the ubiquitous *matryoshka* doll – hollow, colourfully painted wooden figures which fit inside one another to make a family of dolls. Even worse, there were three guys wandering around dressed up as lookalike historical figures, a Stalin, a Lenin and a Gorbachev. I wasn't quite sure what one was supposed to do. Do you give them money and they start making dull speeches, or what? But hey, it was evidence of the tentative emergence of private commerce, and isn't that what we in the West bleat on about all the time? And yet, just a few yards away from all this fakery was a fairly unassuming red marble structure, with a stern-looking guard standing outside. Lenin's Mausoleum. The man himself would be lying in state inside, pickled for all eternity in an open casket like some never-decaying human onion. He was laid to rest there (if you could call it that) for the masses to continue to come and pay homage to the man who had contributed to the founding of the communist ideal. In the end, it didn't quite go as he'd planned and to be honest, he'd somewhat hijacked the whole revolution in the first place, as history shows that the protesting masses had already started the whole thing, before he arrived to take the lead. Nevertheless, I felt compelled to go and see him. There's always something fascinating about death, isn't there? I walked towards the entrance and was immediately challenged by a security man.

'No photos, no talking and take your hat off,' he said gruffly.

This was not to be a typical tourist photo opportunity clearly, and strict reverence was the order of the day. I did as I was told, removing my woolly beanie hat, before entering the mausoleum. It was dark and moody, with only dim wall lights directing my way downwards, until I reached a small, deathly quiet, square room, stark and empty, except for a large glass container set in the middle. And there he was, lying on his back with his eyes closed, on a bed of shiny purple Dracula-like sheets, a much smaller man than you would imagine, with tiny hands and trademark pointy beard. You cannot stare at him for long though, as the security guards usher you along. This was a custom adopted when thousands of Russians would come to pay their respects and had to be moved on quickly, to allow time for others to see. So even though there were only a few curious tourists to deal with, we were still firmly chaperoned along to the exit, after a mere twenty-second viewing. Not that I was expecting him to actually do much, but a few more minutes of gawping would have been nice. Was it really him though, or just a waxwork model? I had heard that every now and then they would take him away to get his skin and body chemically replenished and preserved. What a strange job that would be. A real first date conversation stopper, as your steaks arrive at the table.

'So, what do you do for a living?'

'I inject formaldehyde into people's arteries. Usually dead ones. I have to drain the blood out first though… '

'Oh.'

As I exited the mausoleum after my brief walk-past, I realised that this was a city of contradictions. Opposite the resting place of Lenin, across the other side of Red Square, was a huge glossy and very expensive shopping centre, packed with designer brands, perfumes and gold watches in what was a modern indoor steel and glass emporium; Moscow's attempt to show how connected it was to today's world of commerce. What on earth would the waxwork man behind me have made of it all? With the majority of Russians hardly able to afford their rent and feed themselves, it seemed more like a snub to Lenin and his philosophies. Hardly power to the people. And yet his tomb was still being revered much as it was decades ago. I left Red Square and headed home.

Bang! Bang! Bang!

Someone in the apartment below was hitting something very hard with something very big.

Bang! Bang! Bang!

And then the drilling started.

Rrrr! Rrrr! Rrrrrrrrrrrrr!

Would this ever stop? The answer was no. Renovating apartments is something of a national pastime in Russia. In the West, especially if it's a big job, you plan it. You get some experts to look at the project, you decide the budget and you work out how long it will take. You make sure it's done in such a way as to reduce costs and minimise the time taken to complete it. For an average-sized uncomplicated apartment, it should take a few weeks, if you've done your homework properly. But in Russia it goes on for *years*, with endless trauma and setbacks. This is how a conversation might go in the UK:

'I'm renovating my apartment.'

'Oh, that's great! What are you planning to do to it?'

And here's how the conversation goes in Russia:

'I'm renovating my apartment.'

'Oh, I'm so sorry to hear that. You have our sympathies.'

So why does it take so long in Russia? Well, first of all, many Russians want to upgrade their fixtures and fittings from dark, dank, Soviet boxes, to modern, shiny, Western-style pads. By doing so, they can rent them out at exorbitant cost to foreigners and make a lot of money. Sometimes it's just for their own satisfaction of course. Years of not being allowed to do anything of any real gain, results in people going slightly crazy when given a little freedom. However, renovation doesn't come cheap and many decide to do it themselves. And so it gets done piecemeal, depending on when they have free time, and when they can afford materials. Often though, the old Soviet wiring and plumbing is a sight to behold, and dragging it into the twenty-first century is no mean feat. The result? Endless noise for hapless neighbours over a sprawling amount of time. It just never stops. And for someone like me who would be working different shift patterns, it would be a total nightmare. At once, I realised I had to move, having only been in my new apartment for a matter of days.

Bang! Bang! Bang! Rrrrrrrrrrrrr!

'Oh Cary, no worry! We find better place, my dear. No worry!'

Marina had returned to rescue me from my noise hell, which had just got worse owing to another neighbour beginning nightly practice on an electric guitar, using speakers from the Devil's own rock band.

'We go now,' she said.

And so, to another apartment. This time it was situated in a central area known as Stary Arbat, a pretty, pedestrianised street, full of book fairs, street artists and historical buildings. This long thoroughfare was often the focal point for carnival-type marches and processions, not on the scale of London's Notting Hill Carnival or anything, but nonetheless good-natured events giving Russians a chance to let off some steam.

My apartment was on the sixth floor of a very grand building, consisting of a huge marble entrance, with chandeliers and a 24-hour concierge service. Wow. This was all highly unusual, and the apartment itself was beautiful. High corniced ceilings, tall wrap-around windows with views across Moscow and real pinewood floors. There were so many gadgets in the bathroom and kitchen I didn't know where to start. The funny thing was, it wasn't costing any more than the other place, yet the difference in standard was remarkable. It just shows, in Moscow, you never know.

My landlord was a middle-aged Russian man by the name of Petr. Keenly intelligent and mild-mannered, he spoke pretty good English, and always seemed to have a smile on his wrinkled face, or laughter in his blue eyes. From what I could work out he was divorced and his wife had moved away, leaving him and his ten-year-old son living in a massive apartment right next to mine. Petr invited me in for a welcoming drink. The first thing that struck me was the size of his place. It must have had at least ten rooms, and I mean ten *big* rooms, all ranged across two sides of the block. The second thing I noticed were all the religious pictures and murals hanging on nearly every available space on the walls. Here was a man who took his godliness seriously. The most widespread religion in Russia is Orthodox Christianity and Petr was clearly an enthusiast, if you can call it that. Gold-coloured images of Jesus, Mary, the Apostles, fat flying cherubs and others were all carefully arranged so as to be visible as soon as you entered a room or turned a corner.

'Would you like some vodka?' enquired Petr.

(Did Jesus approve of vodka?)

'Thanks, yes.'

The truth was I hadn't yet tried Russian vodka, so this would be my induction into a beverage so relentlessly associated with Russians, that I couldn't imagine a Russian being much more than a few strides away from a tipple. Petr retrieved two small glass tumblers and a bottle of fearsome-looking Russian-labelled vodka. But before he poured, he went to the fridge and came back with some black bread and what looked like pickled gherkins. This, I was to discover, was highly traditional and I soon realised that the vodka had to be taken neat.

'Do you have any orange juice to mix with it?' I asked.

Petr gave me a withering look. Clearly this was sacrilege of some kind.

'No,' he said flatly. According to him, there was no reason for a real man to add orange juice, tomato juice or any other silly notion. And in any case, he didn't have any. Here then was a real test of my willingness to engage in new cultural experiences. Petr poured and we clinked tumblers. The vodka was unforgivingly strong, though I noticed how easily he was downing his, while the merest sip on my part felt like fire. The bread and gherkins were just bystanders in all this, as the traditional Russian tipple of ages showed me in no uncertain terms that here was a custom not to be messed with and certainly never to be outdone.

I asked Petr what he did for a living. After all, a man who owned an apartment this big (ten rooms!) and as it turned out several other apartments in Moscow, including the one I was renting from him, must be affluent to say the least. He replied somewhat evasively that he was a 'businessman'. Well, that could mean anything, and I suspected that he was actually part of the ruling elite who basically did nothing. Maybe the head of a state-controlled steel company or gas firm. The sort of person who could just sit around all day and watch his bank account getting bigger and bigger, without actually doing anything to make it so. Either way, he quickly changed the subject.

'Why have you come to Moscow?' he asked.

This was a question I had already been asked many times; the people I had met seemed genuinely surprised that anyone would want to come and live here, over London or Milan or New York, say. It was as if they had not quite come to terms with the fact that Moscow was indeed an international city too. They seemed convinced that anyone who came here must be slightly unhinged. And perhaps I was.

'Well, I have come for work and also to explore Russia,' was my stock answer to this and it seemed to satisfy.

He continued to pour me shots of vodka at an alarming rate, as he showed me how to devour the combination correctly. First the gherkin, then the vodka, then the bread. Or was it the vodka, bread and then the gherkin? My head was beginning to spin, not just with the alcohol, but also the whirlwind experience I had put myself through in the last few days. Images were running through my head – the snowy arrival at the airport, the helpful army man, Red Square and, of course, the extraordinary cold. I was no nearer to understanding the Russians than I was when I arrived, but it was early days. Hopefully that would come in time. Living abroad is harder than most people imagine and I was willing to forgive myself for concentrating mostly on finding somewhere to live and preparing myself for work.

As I looked at Petr I realised that I no longer knew what he was saying. His lips were moving, his eyes were twinkling and he was smiling and pouring vodka, but it was like watching a foreign film without subtitles – you get the gist of it from the pictures, but the precise meaning is elusive. I was looking at him through a vodka-fuelled haze that was getting thicker every minute. I decided it was time to go back to my apartment, which after all was only a few feet away next door, thank goodness. I had a vague memory of Petr escorting me to my front door, shaking hands and saying goodbye. I then found myself sprawled out on my sofa, looking out at the view of the metropolis from the wrap-around windows of my new bachelor pad, which I was hoping to put to good use. My head was a merry-go-round and my vision was blurring, but it didn't matter. I allowed a smile to break out on my face, because I was proud of what I had achieved thus far. After all, I had survived my first week in Moscow. I passed out.

I awoke to a headache of biblical proportions. Why always the Bible? Why not of Koran-like proportions? Or of *The Great Dune Trilogy* proportions? The morning light was streaming in from the windows, causing me to squint and turn away. I was still on my sofa, but at some point in the night I must have unknowingly vomited on the floor and down my shirt. Horrible. I remembered that this had happened once before, back in what I liked to call my playboy days whilst living in London. I had been partying one night in the West End and had become so inebriated with champagne and cocktails that on the way home I was forced to exit the London Underground one stop before my destination, in order to puke up in a nearby park. I remembered lying there face down until morning, still wearing the previous night's gladrags, when I was awoken by a dog licking my vomit-covered face and a distant voice crying, 'Benji! Leave him alone! Leave the poor man alone!' I could feel Benji's smelly doggy tongue rasping against my cheek and his breath panting in my ear, but I was still in such a state that I didn't even have the energy to do anything about it. I just lay there being licked in the face by the mutt, until his owner grabbed his lead and took him away from the 'poor man' (whilst making no attempt to check on my condition – that's the big city for you). Surely my lowest point, never to be repeated. Yet, here I was wallowing in my own sick again, in another capital city, this time with bits of half-digested vodka-smelling gherkin sticking to my shirt. No dog this time, but pretty bad nonetheless. Ugh.

I shuffled to the bathroom, cleaned myself up and took stock of the situation. I was to start my new job the next day, so needed to get myself together. You may think that television is a glamorous environment. Well, it isn't really. It has the same egos, tensions and back-stabbing as any other workplace in any other industry. The only people who think television is glamorous are the people who are trying to get into it. Those on the inside soon discover that you don't last long if you take it too seriously. Never believe your own publicity, as they say. You are not the star of the show. The *show* is the star of the show. And let's be clear, I'm no celebrity.

So, my first day at work was like any other person's first day at work. You meet everyone and instantly forget their names. You get shown where everything is and later get lost in the maze. You are taught how the computer system works and then make a mess of it later. You take several loo breaks just to get away for a few moments. And you have a constant smile on your face to try and make all your new colleagues like you, which by the end of the day is making your jaw ache. And at the end of it all, you are exhausted with all the meeting and greeting, even though in work terms you've actually done nothing at all. There were a few differences, though, that made this workplace particularly Russian. For example, I noticed that Russian men had the odd habit of relentlessly shaking hands with one another. And I don't mean guys they have just met, but all the men they already knew too. If you passed the same bloke in the corridor five times in a day, you would still have to stop and shake his hand every single time. On a busy day, it could take all day to get from one end of the building to the other. Yet strangely, the same did not apply for women. Women didn't shake hands. Even when I met them for the first time it still didn't happen, and many a time I found my extended hand simply blowing in the wind, while having to embarrassingly retract my business-like greeting. Clearly, Russia was something of a man's world.

The RT building was a huge oblong concrete block right in the centre of town. Inside, the newsroom itself was an open-plan affair, hosting a sprawl of computer terminals, lots of keen young Russian and British journalists tapping away at their desks, and TV monitors on the walls showing pictures from other news channels across the world. As I entered the room, many of the journalists looked up, probably wondering who on earth I was and what I would be doing. I noticed a spattering of American accents too and even a Kiwi (not Australian, as he later pointed out). There was the usual group of IT geeks in the corner (why are they always such misfits?), the programme directors at the front, some producers to the side, a couple of coffee machines, guest sofas and a general buzz that you would expect in any newsroom. *And a lot of very stunning Russian women.* This brings me on to something, which simply cannot be avoided when the subject of Russia comes up in any conversation. When a Westerner thinks of Russia, they think of vodka, snow, the Gulag, bears, funny hats and… 'Russian brides'. I made a mental note to quiz my colleagues later about Russian women and the male attitude towards womankind here. For now, it was all I could do to stop staring at these girls and maintain a professional demeanour. Get a grip, man.

'Come this way,' said my guide for the day, a young woman by the name of Oksana, with a blonde, neatly trimmed horizontal fringe and very long hair. It seemed that most of the Russians that worked there were bilingual, but in all honesty, I was hardly concentrating on what she was saying. Her eyes were as blue and sparkly as sapphires, as corny as that sounds. Before then I had thought the word 'sparkly' could only be attributed to people's eyes in fairy-tale books, yet here was someone who possessed them for real. I was entranced, and practically falling over with embarrassed awkwardness.

She led me to the office of the news director, the very man who had interviewed me just a few weeks before in London. I entered Alexey's office to find him sitting at his desk, scrutinising a document on his computer.

'Yes, sit, sit,' he said, gesturing to the chair on the other side of the desk. It seemed to me that my chair was a little lower than his. I may have imagined it of course, but it's a favourite tactic used by bosses around the world. Give the employee a smaller and lower chair and he or she is likely to be a bit smaller and lower in what they have to say. This was definitely the case of a certain infamous BBC News boss I recalled. A straight-talking, no-nonsense kind of guy who knew how to intimidate, and then some. Legend has it that when well-known and confident correspondents came into his sixth-floor office and started demanding better pay and conditions, he would deal with them without mercy – something like this:

Correspondent: 'I think my reports speak for themselves, I work very hard and have not had a meaningful pay rise for at least two years. I think I am within my rights to request one.'

Boss: (stares at correspondent in silence).

Correspondent: 'Er… well… what do you think?'

Boss: (after long pause) 'Stand up and go to the window.'

Correspondent: 'Pardon…?'

Boss: 'You heard me.'

At this point, the confused correspondent would rise and walk to the window.

Boss: 'Look outside.'

The correspondent would look out at the drab, grey, typically British wintry scene stretching to the horizon, with only bare trees breaking up the concrete landscape, and the mass of downtrodden people shuffling along the pavement.

Boss (in a whisper): 'It's cold out there, isn't it?'

Well, if the man sitting in front of me wanted to intimidate in a similar manner, he certainly had his own style, as hanging above the window behind him was a huge Kalashnikov automatic rifle. Bloody hell. I suspected it was more for show and amusement than any actual shooting of correspondents, but either way it certainly gave the BBC guy a run for his money.

'It's real, you know,' said Alexey with a proud glint in his eyes, observing my wide-eyed surprise. And trust me, I was not for a second going to doubt his veracity on the issue. Though actually, Alexey turned out to be a lot less harsh away from the interview situation where I had first met him, and rather likeable.

'Hope you're settling in,' he said.

'Yes, great thanks.'

And that was more or less it. Except for one last thing before I began my shifts. Alexey told me he was taking me to meet the editor-in-chief of the channel. The woman who would become one of the most influential people in the global media world. The woman who was personally appointed to her position by Vladimir Putin himself. The woman whose reputed confidence in her abilities and the channel's mission were said to be unwavering to the point of obsession. Margarita Simonyan. Or 'Madge' as she was known somewhat cheekily by the foreigners at the TV station. Her meteoric rise to the top at the comparatively young age of twenty-five, coupled with her unusually close friendship to Putin, always begging the question: 'Did they or didn't they?' Who the heck knows? And in any case, would such questions arise if she was a man rather than a woman? Probably not.

I was ushered by Alexey into her office. By top dog standards, her office was relatively modest. Nothing too flashy. No personal knick-knacks on show. Just a large three-sided wooden desk.

'This is Cary Johnston, he's starting today,' said Alexey,

who then spent the next few minutes staring downwards, without a word.

I greeted her and shook her hand. She was a woman of Armenian complexion and darting eyes.

'So why did you take the job?' she asked, her steady voice giving nothing away.

I gave my usual explanation about travel and work, but found myself wondering what she was actually about, as I couldn't quite fathom her. She seemed somewhat guarded. The meeting lasted no longer than five minutes, before Alexey was ushering me out. A few weeks later though, I was to meet her again at an RT documentary programme launch party, where she was far more personable, approachable and easy-going. I guess she was just more relaxed outside of work (aren't we all?). It was to be the last time our paths would cross, so if you're looking for some personal insights into the character and motivation of the RT channel's editor-in-chief, I'm not your man.

The next day I was in the studio reading my first news bulletin. When you have a slow day at work, time seems to take ages to pass, but when you are busy, it zips by in a shot. Luckily I had a busy shift, with interviews, live reports and all the other stuff that makes up a TV news bulletin. There were a few Russian names I would have to brush up on (it is not *Vladi-meer Putin*, but more like *Vla-dee-meer Putin*, with the emphasis on the second syllable) and many words that as a Westerner I would always have trouble with, but practice makes perfect, or as near as dammit. Before I left for home, I met one of my fellow workers, a chap by the name of George. Now George was what you would call a 'good egg'. A man who was as helpful, welcoming and friendly as you could possibly want. A tallish, well-spoken patriotic English gentleman type, whose motto could easily have been 'for Queen and country'. George enjoyed good company, good red wine and good times. An intelligent, ruffle-haired energetic type, he was curious about everyone and everything, and was a good listener. I never quite got to the bottom of why he had decided to live in Moscow, but then people would often wonder the same about me. Let's face it, Russia Today was giving us work and paying us for it – which was more than could be said for most of the media in the UK at the time. I looked at George and decided it was time to cut to the chase. I was, after all, a single bachelor.

'So, what's the score with Russian women then?' I asked.

George smiled.

'If you want to know the answer to that, you'll have to find out yourself,' he said cryptically. 'Tonight, we hit the town.'

Here we go!

2

THE OLDEST PROFESSION

'In darkest midwinter with two feet of snow on the ground,
Russian women would still be wearing their high heels'

It was to be my first proper night out in Moscow and I was very excited. Like any city, you need to hook up with someone in the know to really get under the skin of a place. It turned out that by coincidence, I was now living on the same street as George. So we simply met outside my apartment, which thankfully was in a much less dodgy part of town than the hotel I had endured, and we went on to an Irish-themed pub nearby. Like all Irish-themed pubs around the world, there was not much that was Irish about it, but the bar was friendly enough and it was a good place to start the evening. It was there that I met another work colleague by the name of Conor, a larger than life

Irish intellectual whose knowledge of Irish history and contemporary politics was mind-boggling. A thickset burly individual, he entered the pub wearing a bohemian black-brimmed hat over a shock of grey wiry hair, newspapers in hand and a book of poetry tucked under his arm, with an overly long scarf draped nonchalantly around his neck in the manner of Tom Baker from the science-fiction series *Doctor Who*. Conor liked to hold court and goodness could he tell a story. He could keep you in stitches for hours with hysterical monologues about life in Ireland, or an anecdote about someone he had just met in the street. He seemed to spend a fair amount of time chasing Russian women, and he also swore a lot.

'How's it feckin' goin'?' he asked in his Irish lilt.

'All good,' I said. 'I'm looking forward to my first adventure.'

'Ah, there'll be plenty feckin' more.'

After a couple of pints, we all three headed round the corner to another drinking haunt by the name of *Zhiguli* (pronounced like *Gigolo*, but with an 'ee' on the end, so like *Gigo-lee*). As is the case outside most bars and clubs in Moscow, there were two aggressive-looking doormen. This is what in Russia is called *Feis Kontrol*. If they don't like your face, you would not be getting in. They would literally control your face by putting a fist in it, if they thought you were a troublemaker. Though actually, it was really if they didn't like your *shoes*. Indeed, the first thing these two brutes did was look at my shoes. In their minds, if I was wearing a decent pair it meant that I was well-heeled, and thus worth letting in. Also, the slush and snow was such that if you walked too far in good shoes it just messed them up, ruining the foot of your trousers. But if I was really a person who had money to burn, then why would I be walking in the snow in the first place? Why wouldn't I have paid for a taxi? So clean shoes and clean trouser bottoms equalled a big wallet, or such was the logic that went through a Moscow bouncer's head when considering if a person was suitable to be admitted. In actual fact, just being a foreigner was normally sufficient, as it was generally perceived by the locals that foreigners had plenty of cash to spend, and although we were not millionaires, we were wearing smart Western clothes. Also, men were more likely to be admitted into places than women. The logic was that men have the money and demographically there were far fewer men than women in Moscow, so it was generally a good idea to let the males in. This of course is the opposite in the West, where getting into a nightclub as a group of males was nigh impossible, as you would be considered to be potential troublemakers. So, with a silent nod of the head from the heavies on the door, we were in. The first thing we had to do was go through the ritual of shedding layers and layers of clothing. Without them, you would freeze outside, but it meant you had to spend ages taking everything off – gloves, hats, scarves, jumpers, coats, whatever – and handing them over to the cloakroom attendant. Every bar and club had a cloakroom, and every cloakroom had an attendant, and every attendant would pretend the cloakroom was full until you handed over a one hundred rouble tip. The look of total honesty on their faces as they told you it was full, would have befitted any Oscar-winning performance. Yet when you passed over the money, the complete lack of guilt at having deceived you was another stage classic.

Now on first inspection this *Zhiguli* place just looked like a restaurant with big tables and white tablecloths everywhere, subdued lighting, gentle piped music and a central bar area. Groups of Russians were already tucking into what looked like quite decent grub. But as the evening progressed, the music became louder and everyone started dancing around the tables and later *on* the tables. Let me make it quite clear – Russian men cannot dance; the women can, but the men can't. Nonetheless they like to have a go, and with a few vodkas neatly dispatched, there's no stopping them. The music was basically what you would describe as 1980s, but that's 1980s Russia, not Wham! or Sinitta or Billy Ocean. Instead, it was a cross between a German oompah band and Europop. Relentlessly rubbish, yet they loved it and I couldn't help wanting to join in too. So dance we did. As far as I could tell, we were the only foreigners in the place, which is why George and Conor had taken me there, to experience a real Russian dance club. We were certainly attracting a lot of attention from the Russian women, and my God, there were lots of them, far outnumbering the men. This was a real change of environment, compared to having a night out in Britain. Here, it was easier to get in and there was very little competition from other men, basically because there were hardly any in the first place. One thing I learnt very quickly though, was that women in Russia do not buy anything on an evening out. Ever. You as the male are paying for all the drinks, all the food, all the taxis and all the tips.

As the evening and dancing continued, I wondered about all these stunning-looking girls who were staring at us. Their hair and nails, perfect. Their matching bags and shoes, perfect. Their catwalk model poise, perfect. Were they just having 'a laugh' and enjoying the 'craic' as my new-found Irish friend Conor would have put it? Or were they instead a group of cynical preying felines all looking for a foreigner to sink their claws into, with the hope of getting married quickly and emigrating to the West? I felt terrible even thinking that, given how friendly and warm everyone had been thus far. But we in the West have been conditioned to think badly of Russian girls. Well, here was the chance to discover if they were all indeed just potential Russian brides. We've all heard of this of course. Young women who put themselves onto mail order lists via the internet in order to attract some wholly inadequate middle-aged pot-bellied Western male, who probably has more money than sense, tricking him into marriage and then dumping him the moment something better comes along. Or so the story goes. Was this true?

I was to discover that in some instances there was an element of truth to this, but it didn't tell the whole story. Certainly many Russian women were, objectively, extraordinarily beautiful. Obviously beauty is in the eye of the beholder, but in my humble opinion the women of Asia, the Caribbean, North or South America, Africa, Western Europe, Australasia, hell anywhere else in the *world*, had nothing over the women of Russia. It was not just their extraordinary style and finesse. Or their perfectly fitting and co-ordinating clothes. Or the gemstone-like intensity of their eyes. No, it was more than that. It was the completely disarming *naturalness* of their demeanour that made them irresistible to doe-eyed Western males. And all this within the most meagre of circumstances. The average Russian female earned around one hundred pounds a month, hardly enough to pay for rent and food, let alone designer clothes and perfumes. So instead, they simply made do with what they had, but in frugal ways, which would have put a church mouse to shame. Somehow everything they wore looked exquisite. Every nuance of make-up was entrancing. And every movement and gesture they made was unashamedly female. It just *worked*. They also spent a lot of time in front of mirrors. Russian girls and mirrors were like moths to a light. If you got into a lift that contained a mirror within, they would stand in front of it preening their hair to the extent that they barely remembered to get out at the right floor. If a Russian woman came to your apartment, she would spend the most unfathomably long time in the bathroom doing… what?

Any time, day or night, no matter how tired they were, or how early it was, or even if it was just to pop out for the weekly food shop, Russian girls would present themselves as though they had just stepped out of a photo shoot. In deepest, darkest midwinter with two feet of snow on the ground, Russian women would still be wearing their high heels, I kid you not. There even reached a point where I thought to myself, 'Oh, for God's sake give it a *rest* and wear a pair of trainers, you've only come out for five minutes to post a letter.' And before you accuse me of blatant sexism with all this, I assure you it is not just the ramblings of some sad Western male howling like a wolf with his tongue on the floor. Take Mimi, a sophisticated British photographer friend of mine who came to visit me in Moscow for a few days later that month. She had never been to Moscow before and as we sauntered down the street towards Red Square, she suddenly blurted out what was on her mind.

'My God, there's a lot of hotties around. Look at her, and her, and *her*.'

I told her to imagine she was living in a place where every man looked like Pierce Brosnan, or George Clooney, or Colin Firth, or that bloke from *Pirates of the Caribbean*, whatshisname. It would be brilliant for a while, but if you started going out with Pierce and then George passed you by in the street, you'd be forgiven for turning your head and thinking, 'Hey, he's pretty cute.' Not only that, but George is giving you that 'I understand your pain' look in his eyes. And then Pierce takes you to a restaurant and on the next table Johnny Depp (that's the Pirate bloke's name, isn't it?) starts giving you a cheeky smile and surreptitiously passes you his phone number. Then as you get up to go to the ladies' room, Jude Law appears from nowhere and presents you with a huge bouquet of impossibly vibrant and beautiful red roses. And as you walk back to the table where Pierce is waiting (remember him?) an immaculately dressed Orlando Bloom asks if you would like to join him at the bar for a drink of vintage champagne, and in that moment Colin Firth has just texted you asking if you'd like to go for a romantic walk in the park. Because in this mythical place, not only are all the men fantastically good-looking, but they are all attainable and they all seem to want you. I mean, where does it all end? How do you choose between Pierce, George, Johnny, Jude, Orlando, Colin and all the rest of them? A sea of eligible, gorgeous, intelligent, interesting, single men. *Well that's what it's like in Moscow*. Only substitute the above men for women, and swap the lucky recipient of all that attention for foreign men who just happen to be living in Russia. Even in my brief time in the newsroom thus far, I remembered two guys discussing this issue, when suddenly a female British news desk journalist chipped in.

'If I were a foreign man living in Moscow, I wouldn't bother getting married. I mean there are so many gorgeous women to shag you'd be wasting your time hitching up with just one, wouldn't you?' she said half-jokingly to her stunned male audience.

Looks aside, how did this inequality of numbers come about? (I reckoned the count was about four to one in the club, in favour of women). Well, let's go back in time a little. Due to his unending paranoia of plots against him, Soviet dictator Joseph Stalin purged millions of Russians, mainly men. Then during the Second World War, a further ten million men as I've said before were thrown at Hitler's forces. Their role in defeating the Germans should not be underestimated. This was less to do with Stalin's panache as a military tactician, and more due to the fact that there were so many Russians willing to die to save their country from being overrun by Nazis.

Then on the break-up of the Soviet Union in the early '90s, tens of thousands of Russian men emigrated to Western Europe, looking for work. It was deemed as far easier for men to find employment than women. The aim was to eventually return, which many never did. Also, male life expectancy in Russia is significantly lower than that of women, because they smoke and drink too much. So it's clear that in less than a generation, something like a fifth of the male population if not more, had in one way or another, disappeared. In short, there weren't enough men around, but there were still an awful lot of women. But how would this affect the demographics a generation on? Why would the fewer men that were left all start producing girls and not boys? Well, it is said that male Russian sperm tends to produce more females than males because it becomes damaged in some way by their poor lifestyle and that the male chromosome is more prone to damage than the female one. In other words, toxic sperm. I had no idea if this was scientifically sound or not, but what I did know was that there were a lot more women than men around town. If you are a geneticist feel free to argue my point, but let me tell you there were nights I would go to bars and be *surrounded* by women, with not a bloke in sight. I've probably glossed over a few other demographic reasons for all this, but that's the gist of it. Hence, the women had to fight for attention. In a basic sense, if the women didn't make themselves stand out they had no chance of getting a bloke, let alone a decent, well-mannered, generous, polite sort of bloke, but just *any* sort of bloke. And then add into this gender mix the sudden arrival of Western men who had come to live and work in the new Russia, and you had a cocktail of sexual chemistry, which inevitably led to a lot of hanky-panky. Don't forget that Russia only opened up to the West in terms of work and business after the collapse of the Soviet Union. Before that, there was nothing. No fancy restaurants, no sophisticated bars, no Western-style discos, no Starbucks, no bottled Corona beer with a bit of lime stuck on top, no consumerism that you and I take for granted, and no communication with the outside world, except for the very privileged few. It's hard for us to comprehend, but when I asked a similarly-aged Russian work colleague about her memories of the internationally groundbreaking Live Aid concert at Wembley in 1985, she replied, 'What's Live Aid? Sir Bob Geldof? Who's he…?'

Many of the Western cultural references which I assumed everyone was privy to, had not even touched the people of the biggest country in the world. It meant that the Western male was very much an exotic creature to them. Seemingly gentlemanly, well travelled, well dressed and apparently loaded with cash. Certainly, compared to the average Russian man's salary, the Western interloper was virtually a millionaire. And boy, do Russian women like receiving presents. Bags, shoes, earrings, you name it, they wanted it. And why not?

I am generalising now, but compare this to the somewhat rough-and-ready nature and appearance of Russian men, who never seemed to even notice their female compatriots. For them, pretty women were the norm and what's so amazing about the norm? Hence, they didn't appear to appreciate or revere the women of their land as much as we did. Familiarity breeds complacency at best, contempt at worst. So Russian women wanted Western men and Western men wanted Russian women. A match made in heaven. Or hell, depending on your point of view, as I was to discover in *Zhiguli*.

Let's talk for a moment about 'the oldest profession'. And I ask you to suspend your possibly entrenched views on the following subject, in the interests of *understanding* – though you may not ultimately be in agreement. With that caveat duly noted, here goes: The *Oxford English Dictionary* definition of the word 'prostitute' is 'a person who has sex for money'. Seems pretty simple and straightforward, but when I applied it to Russia, things seemed to get a tad blurred. Wind forward a little: when I went to any nightclub like *Zhiguli*, there would be the usual bewildering array of gorgeous Russian females, most just out for a good time with friends, having a dance, having a laugh, that sort of thing. There also seemed to be – which quickly became unsettling – a good number of prostitutes. *Or were there*?

Away from the clubs, there was a certain minority of women who had normal (though badly paid) jobs, normal lives, normal families, yet were also willing it seemed to jump into bed 'on the side' as it were, to make a bit of extra cash. They didn't do it full-time, just whenever it suited, and without the need for pimps. Did that make them prostitutes? Well, according to the definition I had found earlier, yes it did. So let's continue.

These women found it impossible to get good jobs. You may think that your Western workplace is often sexist. You may think that your company has discriminatory attitudes towards women looking for employment, or inequality when it comes to pay. Well, that's nothing compared to what I discovered in Moscow. Russia was such a man's world, that in the past some job application adverts apparently included the phrase 'without complications'. A code phrase meaning, 'You may have to sleep with the boss on a regular basis if you want this job.' Can you imagine? Now, add to that the additional economic hardship in the form of a Russian financial crisis and a case of being unable to travel to another country to look for work due to severe visa restrictions. In those circumstances, and when you have been culturally conditioned from birth to believe that this is how it is, what is a Russian woman to do? As I've said before, their wages in roubles were often pitiful, and so some (not all, I hasten to add!) turned to 'the oldest profession' which in Russia was not illegal in the past (though it is now) and as such, has none of the stigma attached to it that we are familiar with. I'm not saying they liked it, but this practice was not manifestly controlled by gangs and most of it was purely down to the girl herself. Is it still prostitution? Well, yes it is… isn't it?

The interesting thing is that most women in Russia care most about one thing – security. That someone buys them presents, clothes, takes them out for dinner, offers them a place to stay and keeps them safe. They don't care if that person is their boyfriend, husband or some stupid expat tourist. Only that they are looked after. Many even lived in central Moscow apartments paid for by some bloke who had a wife and kids outside the city and only came in once a month for a bit of sexual indiscretion. Did these women feel dirtied by this? I can honestly say, apparently not. For some Russian women, a relationship with a Russian man was more like a contract: 'I will look pretty and have a relationship with you, while you will pay for everything and take me to nice places and expensive restaurants, forever and ever. Amen. Sign here.'

So what kind of society is that? Well, a brutally honest one I suppose, but also a somewhat disturbing one for a foreigner. It makes the life of an expat male rather uncomfortable. On the one hand you don't want to be dragged down into anything that could be called 'prostitution'. On the other hand, how else are you to have a relationship with a female here? Not only that, but in the case of a Western male the contract is slightly amended: 'I will look pretty and have a relationship with you, while you will pay for everything and take me to nice places and expensive restaurants, forever and ever. Amen. Oh, and as you're from the West, you will also marry me and take me with you when you eventually leave. We will then have kids and live happily ever after. Sign here.' Many Westerners would see this as predatory. Many from Eastern Europe would see it as simply practical. Can love also be involved in this 'contract'? Well, of course it can. It's just that initially, it comes a bit further down on the list of requirements. In any case, this did not apply to *all* Russian women – that would be a gross generalisation of course. But nevertheless, I had seen what I had seen. I am not, I hasten to add, talking about or even vaguely condoning the abhorrent gang-related trafficking of women across Russian borders or anywhere else, for the purposes of modern slavery and sexual exploitation. That evil is self-evident. Nor am I suggesting that Russian women are all prostitutes. That would be patently untrue and unfair. No, I am attempting to describe something else, something more cultural and elusive…

Let's wind back now to the *Zhiguli* club. So there I was at the bar, with George and Conor chatting away to a posse of Russians at one end, and me on my own clutching a vodka and orange at the other (you should have seen the barman's look of pity as I poured the orange juice into the vodka). The forever inquisitive George was already exchanging business cards, while Conor was holding court with a group of Russian women, giving them a tall story about how Rasputin was related to an Irish guy from Donegal, or something or other. The Russians were lapping it up, while insisting he downed ever more rapidly appearing shots of vodka – clapping each successful 'down in one' with whoops of delight and applause. As I turned round, a young girl said something in Russian to me. She was pretty and well turned out (weren't they all?), slim and petite. Blue eyes and honey-blonde hair. I had already learnt one invaluable Russian phrase.

'*Vy gavariti pa-angliski?*' (Do you speak English?)

'A little,' she replied in a sexy Russian accent, batting her eyelashes. Another rule of engagement was that a Russian woman never refuses a drink. Compare that to the dismissive (and often deserved) wave of the hand that you received from Western women and I could see why this place was a male paradise. After years of rejection conditioning though, it still took a while to pluck up the courage and I was pleasantly surprised when she nodded her head in approval.

'Of course,' she smiled. 'I'm Tatiana.'

The lack of variety of women's names in Russia was incredible; so far I had only come across about seven. And there was also a very strict tradition of how women could be named, with all women's names ending with an 'a'. So everyone was called something like Natalia, Svetlana, Katya, Marina, Oksana, Olga or Tatiana. So far, I had not found a Russian girl with a silly celebrity name like 'Honey' or 'Clementine' or 'Peaches', for example, though that was probably a good thing. Peaches, the late daughter of Sir Bob Geldof and the late TV presenter Paula Yates, once reportedly complained that at school she was constantly teased by other pupils with shouts of, 'Oi Peaches! Are your parents Bananas?' Poor girl.

I turned my attention to the drinks menu, while Tatiana regarded me expectantly. Now, there was an alcoholic drink in Russia called *Champanski*. Believe me it was anything but champagne – a sweet, sickly and hideous pretend version of the French original, which had the French champagne houses gnashing their teeth for years, over claims of illegally using their branding.

How Russia had got away with it for so long was anyone's guess. But that was something of the charm of the place; they just do what they like with a shrug of the shoulders and say, 'This is Russia, we can get away with anything.' Nonetheless, I soon wished I had the real thing, as the Russian version had a reputation of making you want to retch at some point in the evening, or soon after your first sip. Worse still, I had been reliably informed that a good deal of drinks served in Russian bars were counterfeit and this *Champanski* hadn't exactly filled me with confidence. I once got served a bottle of Budweiser, with the word 'Budweiser' spelt wrong on the label. However, apart from being substantially cheaper than real champagne, there was one other saving grace that this terrible *Champanski* provided... Russian girls loved it.

As the night progressed, I thought things were going quite nicely with Tatiana and I was beginning to contemplate where the evening might lead.

'Would you like to come back to my apartment for a coffee?' I found myself saying. Did I *really* just say that? Was that the best I could do?

'Yes,' she said.

I went for broke.

'Okay, let's get a taxi and get out of here.'

Unbelievably, it seemed to be working. I said my goodbyes to George and Conor (who both smiled knowingly at me) and shepherded Tatiana to the cloakroom. With coats and accessories collected (including the obligatory ten minutes for her to preen herself in the mirror before departing), we were at my apartment in no time. At that moment, I remembered the age-old saying, 'If it seems too good to be true, it probably is.' But then (stupidly) I ignored that.

'I go wash hands,' said Tatiana, before disappearing to the bathroom for an enormous amount of time, to do whatever it is that Russian girls do in the bathroom. At this point, I will leave to your imagination what happened next. But it was the morning after the night before that the trouble started.

I awoke in a hazy glow to find Tatiana still next to me. I suppose I had had a lingering thought that maybe in the middle of the night she would have drugged me before ransacking the place and taking my wallet or something. But no, all seemed fine, and my credit cards were still in place. She got dressed and prepared to leave. But then a curious thing.

'Maybe shopping now,' said Tatiana in her broken English.

'Sorry?'

'Shopping.'

What on earth did she mean? She shot me a slightly vexed look.

'I need bag and shoes.'

She was talking about shopping? Now? Clearly, she was trying to explain something to me, which I didn't quite understand.

'Present,' said Tatiana.

'Okay, I replied,' still confused. 'We'll go shopping sometime.'

She sighed, before finally leaving, though not before writing down my phone number. I felt slightly perplexed, though still uplifted in a caveman kind of way about the night I had just had. The next day I received a phone call from her.

'We go out?'

'Yeah, great!' I replied enthusiastically.

'But first we meet and we go shopping.'

There was a pause. Then finally the penny dropped. In my naivety I had not realised that Tatiana wanted some kind of remuneration for the night she had spent with me. My heart sank. Didn't this mean that I had been duped by a working girl? Well, in Russia, no. A real prostitute would have agreed a price and taken the money on the night of the dirty deed, wouldn't she? And that had not happened. Also, I imagined (forgive me, but I had not entertained the services of so-called 'ladies of the night' before) that call girls would decide a time limit per transaction – a certain amount of money for a certain amount of time, and the like. But again, this had not happened. Therefore, the only possible conclusion was that she was just a 'normal' girl looking to have some fun, but also to get something tangible out of it in the process. After all, you don't get if you don't ask. Meanwhile, the *Oxford English Dictionary* says nothing about whether a prostitute can be a 'professional' or an 'amateur' or just 'someone who asks for a present every now and then, because they live in Russia, where principles don't pay for accessories'. This was clearly something of a minefield, and one that I did not want to traverse. No money had exchanged hands with Tatiana, and as far as I was concerned, none ever would. But she did expect me to buy stuff. Well, here's the thing. In the UK, if a man pays for dinner on a first date with a woman, does that make his date a prostitute? No, of course not. Well, in Moscow, as well as buying dinner, you are also expected to buy presents. What's the difference? You're still forking out money, aren't you? It's just that in Russia, a new pair of sheepskin-lined leather gloves with matching scarf are that much more useful than just a plate of chicken Kiev and a vanilla crème brûlée. On the other hand, what did I expect in a nightclub? (And what kind of guy did they think *I* was?). Nonetheless, this was clearly going to be an ongoing dilemma.

I declined Tatiana's offer of 'shopping', which led to a stream of abuse down the phone line.

'You are a fucking stupid man!' she shouted.

Funny how her English improved when it came to dishing out expletives. There was more, but I'll leave it at that. I realised that there was no such thing as a 'no strings attached' one-night stand in Russia. Everything had to have some form of remuneration, even in a non-conventional sense. It would also beg the question, 'Does this person really like me, or is she just short of rent for the month?' That kind of question would surely leave a bitter taste in the mouth. In fact, it already had. I wondered if Tatiana eventually found someone else to fund her 'shopping' and just how much 'shopping' money a guy would need to cough up in order to hold down a relationship with a woman here. And in any case, what kind of relationship would that be? A caring monogamous pairing with someone you love? Or just one endless shopping arcade fleecing, in exchange for sex? Questions, questions. And what of all you women back in the UK who have husbands being sent to Eastern Europe and beyond for short business trips – should you be worried? From what I could see, hell yes! Take, for example, a business contact of my new-found mate George. Now George often hosted all manner of friends and business people who were in Moscow for meetings and the like. Often, they would even kip over on his sofa bed, as good hotels were mega-expensive and not everyone was fortunate enough to be on a big 'blow the budget' jolly with their company. And anyway, George liked entertaining. One night, a business colleague of his came over to stay for a few days. To spare this guy's blushes (and the blushes of his wife back in the UK), I shall name him Dick. Probably appropriate given what transpired. A tall, messy-haired, fag-smoking, greasy-looking individual, Dick was in town on legitimate business, trying to put together a corporate deal with some Russians on behalf of his company. But the moment he got into town, Dick's beady eyes were bulging (along with his wayward manhood I imagined).

'Jesus Christ, the totty out here is fucking amazing!' he exclaimed, with the subtlety of a bull in the proverbial china shop, as the three of us went into a bar.

'Oh my God!' was the proclamation at the next bar.

'Fuck me!' was the witty aside as we got to the nightclub. And sure enough, Dick's only intention for the evening was to try to bed almost any Russian girl he could find – which was plenty. Any thoughts for his no doubt long-suffering other half back home were extinguished in a torrent of gushing unstoppable lust. He was determined to get laid. And get laid he did, with a frankly gorgeous twenty-something woman, who was lively, flirty and clearly up for some action (as long as her champagne glass was being replenished on a regular basis, that is). Just one girl in a whole shoal of Russian girlie fish, waiting to be caught in the net of some trawling hungry foreign fisherman. So it was back to the nearest swanky hotel (his personal credit card almost snapping in two with the weight of the bar bill, augmented with the inevitable weight of morning guilt to follow) and straight to action. What was interesting was that Dick was not exactly a handsome chisel-jawed well-dressed hunk of a man. Frankly, he seemed a little ugly to me. And yet as far as I could tell, the woman in question didn't seem to care. He was just a one-night one-man shagathon cash cow.

All of this remained on my mind for the rest of the month as I continued my social whirl of discovering the bars, clubs and restaurants of Moscow. I wasn't just after a relationship (honest), I was also hoping to delve into the Russian psyche, as Moscow was beginning to fascinate me more than any other place I had ever visited. To that end, I wanted to get out and about as much as possible. One evening, while dining at a restaurant with some friends, I was introduced to the French celebrity chef Jean-Christophe Novelli, who was reportedly considering opening a new restaurant in Moscow and was in town for a recce. He and his entourage were sitting at the next table, tucking into some dainty looking nosh and swilling some expensive wine. A tall, good-looking confident kind of guy, sporting a mop of dark hair, Novelli had opened restaurants all over the world and plied his trade not just in kitchens but also on TV shows.

'Come, you sit wiz us,' he offered, in his French accent.

As a bit of an amateur cook myself, I was delighted. The venue was the top floor restaurant at the newly refurbished Hotel Ukraina in central Moscow, a hotel housed within one of the most magnificent buildings in town. Built under Stalin's orders, it was akin to a giant and intricate Gothic skyscraper, lighting up the night sky like some fairy-tale palace. Truly stunning. In fact, there were seven of these buildings, almost identical, scattered across Moscow, collectively known in Russian as *Stalinskie Vysotki*, or in English as the 'Seven Sisters'. The view from the top was quite something and I found Novelli to be disarmingly friendly and reserved, not at all an egocentric foul-mouthed chef that one is given to expect these days. A few others had by this time joined us at the behest of chef Novelli, and an excellent meal was had. In fact, it turned out that he had invited a whole group of people onto the chef's table. Every now and then, immaculately dressed in his white uniform, he would go to the kitchen to survey what was happening before returning to the group, in the manner of a footballer who couldn't resist slinking off to see the highlights of a big game. And at the end of the evening he paid for the entire meal. Can't say fairer than that. Eventually, we said our goodbyes and left the restaurant at around 2am – time flies when you're having fun, especially if someone else is footing the bill. It was then that I had my first experience of Moscow taxis. Up to that point, I had been more than content with using the highly efficient Metro system. But here I was in a place where there were no Metro stations nearby, and in any case they would be closed at this late hour. In the UK, we are constantly lectured by government ministers not to use unlicensed taxis, because they could be dangerous. The drivers have no insurance and possibly no driving licence, meaning that anything could happen to you. We are always told to use proper official licensed black cabs. Though of course everyone still uses unlicensed ones, because an empty black cab is hard to come by at night, and even if you do get one, the driver is usually reluctant to go anywhere further than a few hundred metres away.

'Can you take me south of the River Thames please?'

'South of the river? Sorry mate, it's the end of my shift, can't go that far now.' Or some such excuse.

Basically, they can make a lot more money and tips on three short trips in the affluent West End than on one long one south of the Thames. It also means they save on petrol. I mean, it's all very well government officials telling everyone to take proper cabs; they don't know what it's like waiting in line on a rainy Saturday night. You don't get wet and miserable whizzing by in a chauffeur-driven ministerial Jaguar, do you Minister?

But anyway, in Russia, as was the case with so many things, it was the complete opposite. As I stood by the side of the street, one of my mates put his arm out and within seconds a battered old Lada car, with only one hub cap and a huge dent down the side, swerved to stop next to us. An unkempt-looking guy with a cigarette hanging out of his mouth peered out from within its rickety interior, while using a handle to wind down the window. Not what I would consider, in any shape or form, to be a taxi.

'How much to Arbat?' enquired one of my friends, a squat shaven-headed Dutch guy by the name of Frederick.

'Three hundred roubles.'

'Okay, fine.'

I looked at the ramshackle thing masquerading as a car, and then back at my friends.

'We're not getting into *that* are we? It's not even a taxi, just some punter!'

'Don't worry, it's fine,' they all reassured me.

With three of us crammed into the back and one in the front, I was definitely worried about the safety implications. But then suddenly, two Russian ladies whom Frederick had just met said they wanted to come too.

'Sure, no problem,' he said.

One girl on the lap in the front and one sprawled out across the three of us in the back. Oh my God. And then the 'taxi' sped off, veering across the road like a contestant in *Wacky Races*. Seat belts? Don't be daft, they were probably broken anyway. I was definitely scared, yet everyone was laughing their heads off and I became caught up in the craziness of the whole thing. This is Russian life I thought, as we skidded around the highway. Mad, bad and proud of it!

This kind of 'taxi' was somewhat racistly (is that a word?) known by expats as a 'Gypsy cab'. Apologies to the Roma community, for as far as I could tell, no Romani people were driving them. Either way, we somehow arrived safely and it became clear that there was a whole underclass of jobless Russians and people from central Asia or the Caucasus who basically worked all night as unofficial taxi drivers, using their own vehicles and living off their wits. In fact, you only had to stand too near to the kerb and a whole fleet of 'taxis' would suddenly pile up next to you, all looking for business. And the prices they charged were remarkably cheap. It suddenly opened up a whole new world of entertainment, because the question of how to get home simply never arose. No matter where you were in Moscow you were never more than the equivalent of a six-quid ride home and you never had to wait for a cab. Paradoxically, the 'official' looking Moscow taxis, with their New York-style yellow and black markings, actually charged a fortune and would basically rip you off. Instead, it was always best to look for the most run-down car possible and flag it down, as the driver was more likely to be honest and reliable. The rule was never use a car that looked too expensive; after all, why would someone with an expensive car be looking to pick up a fare? We had all heard tales of foreigners who'd been whisked off to some far-off location to be robbed and beaten, after accepting a lift in a posh-looking car.

So back at my apartment, all six of us adjourned for drinks and frolics. Moscow was turning out to be a twenty-four hour city, and sure enough at 7am we headed out for breakfast to a place called the Starlight Diner, an all-day, all-night American-style hamburger and milkshakes clone, complete with Russian waiters and waitresses wearing stripy red and white uniforms, staggering around in roller skates. The perfect place to recover from alcohol excess, while contemplating the next night's entertainment. Or should I say that night's entertainment, as it was already morning? Who knew? Who cared? I was beginning to fall in love with Moscow. Here was a place where you could do what you wanted, when you wanted, with whom you wanted. It was full of beautiful women and exciting places to discover. I was also getting a feeling that Moscow was a city that had a real edge about it. If you got into trouble there probably wasn't going to be much of a safety net. Yet that in itself raised my awareness and heightened my senses. With the taxis, for example, you had to make an on-the-spot decision from your gut feeling – 'Do I trust this driver or not?' It made you feel alive. The adrenalin never stopped pumping.

So, there were good things and bad things about this place. Thus far, I had sampled only the good, but that gut feeling also told me that I was about to see another side. Like any relationship, falling out of love can happen too. As far as I knew, Novelli never did open a Moscow restaurant during my time there; had something put him off? Was the glitz of this town all that it seemed? As night follows day, the good was about to take a back seat, while the bad was buckling up for some full-on octane-fuelled horror.

3

HORROR

'Here they all were, with hate in their
eyes and vitriol on their lips'

Compared to Western standards, the quality of food in Moscow was not good, and the quality of service in restaurants was almost non-existent. I was in a small Soviet-style eatery one day with a couple of Russian colleagues – simple food served in a no-frills environment, with grey walls sporting a wonky framed picture of some old Soviet leader or other. I decided to order a kind of potato salad with dill for a starter and a fish soup for the main course. One thing I had learnt was that it didn't really matter what you asked for, or in what order it was supposed to come, it all just arrived together – starter, main course, pudding, it didn't matter. It was as though there was no real system going on in the kitchens; everything just arrived as soon as the chef had finished making it, regardless of the table it was destined for. So naturally enough, my main course fish soup arrived along with the potato salad starter all at the same time. The young Russian waiter plonked them down without a word and went off to serve the next hapless customer. I ate the potato dish as fast as I could, before turning my attention to the main course soup, but it was no use – the soup was now cold. I summoned the waiter, before using my best polite British reserved manner.

'Um... excuse me, is there any chance at all you could possibly take the soup back and reheat it for me? You see it's gone a little bit cold whilst I was eating the starter, so I was wondering if you could help me in this respect.'

We Brits are so ridiculously polite. A Yank would have yelled, 'Hey, buddy, you gonna take this back, or what?' Either way, the response from the Russian waiter came like an unwavering short-range ballistic missile.

'Well, it was warm when I brought it,' he replied stony-faced, before simply walking away.

It certainly put me in my place and I left it at that, devouring the insipid liquid in the manner of a prisoner who knows that cold soup is better than no soup. My Russian colleagues just shrugged their shoulders. Later during the same meal, I tried my luck ordering a glass of lemonade. It arrived just fine, but I fancied some ice with it.

'Excuse me (here we go again) can you bring me some ice for my drink please?'

The waiter came across and *put his hand around my glass.*

'Well, it feels cold enough to me,' he said, his face again betraying not a flicker of emotion as he casually walked away again. I looked at my colleagues – more shoulder shrugging.

When McDonald's opened its first outlet in Moscow in 1990, thousands queued for literally miles down the street. For them, it wasn't just the thought of a burger in a bun which excited them so, it was as much the feeling of actually experiencing a part of Western culture that so captivated them. This was a country where up until then, the average person could only get a glimpse of the outside world. Before the collapse of the Soviet Union, no one was allowed out of the country and no one was allowed in, and the same applied to culture and goods. If you wanted to buy some clothes, you had to go to a vast warehouse where poorly made clothes were spread across huge tables. They were grey, drab and uniform. The trouser section would be a vast section of exactly the same trousers. The blouse section would be a vast section of exactly the same blouses, and so on. No variation in colour and style. If you went to a bakery, there would be one type of bread at one price. If you went to the milk shop, there would be one type of milk at one price. Due to the deficiencies of the Soviet transport system, however, these goods would often not arrive, leading to vast queues of people waiting for the next batch. As a result, when Russians were lucky enough to be offered a loaf of bread, they would hand over their money and be eternally grateful.

'*Spasibo, spasibo,*' (Thank you, thank you) they would mutter to the dismissive shop owners (if you could call them that, in a land where no one really owned anything). And so it came to be that whoever had the food could be as rude and supercilious as they liked, because in Soviet society there was no competition. The customers would always come, because they had no choice – there was nowhere else to go. Either put up with the miserable bread seller, or go hungry. And that state of mind seemed to have survived. As such, the advent of a fast food joint was a revelation. Fast, quick service, with a choice of menu! Gasp! But even now, there were still problems. A friend at my workplace had once applied for a job at that same McDonald's. All the staff had undergone a training course in how to serve customers. One day their trainer was explaining the benefits of being polite and friendly to the paying public when a young Russian trainee put his hand up at the back of the class.

'Yes, Andrei,' said the teacher.

'I don't understand,' frowned Andrei, with a quizzical look on his face.

'What don't you understand?'

'Why do we have to be polite and friendly to customers?'

'Because then, they'll be happy to come back again and tell all their friends how good the food and service is here.'

Andrei considered this for a moment.

'But I still don't understand.'

'What don't you understand?'

'Who cares what they think? They will still come back.'

'Why will they come back if they received poor service?' the trainer countered.

(Pause).

'Because we've got the burgers,' reasoned Andrei.

A lingering throwback to Soviet times and an attitude that was particularly ingrained in Russian corner shops. In the UK, the corner shop is often a place you go to not just for the convenience of it being near your home – literally around the corner – but because the shopkeepers have more time to be friendly to you and build up a trusted relationship. In Moscow, however, it makes no difference. Surliness abounds, and no matter how often I went into my local corner shop and no matter how much stuff I bought, the owner still followed me round the aisles as though I was about to steal as many tomatoes and gherkins as I could stuff down my trousers. They also hate it if you don't give them the exact change. One day, the local store owner actually started shouting at me because I had given her a one hundred rouble note for a bottle of water that cost sixty-five roubles. Hardly a problem you would think, but she was adamant that she had no change. At that point, I had had enough, so I just stood my ground.

'I have no change either,' I said, thinking that she would buckle under my tough stance. But with grim steeliness, she simply reached for two packets of chewing gum and a packet of crisps and threw them down next to the bottle of water. In other words, she was instructing me to buy more items so she would not have to give me any change. Truly amazing!

'You can keep your pissing water!' I fumed, grabbing my money back and vowing never to return.

Department stores, too, displayed no subtlety when it came to things like security. The store security guards would stand outside the entrance doors like nightclub bouncers, eyeballing you as soon as you entered, making no pretence of their suspicions. I was once in a large supermarket that had eighteen checkouts. However, as it was very early in the day, only one checkout was open and I was the only customer at that checkout. It should have been plain sailing and yet it soon turned into an unexpected conflict. The security guard at the other end of the store made it his job to walk all the way from checkout number one to stand right next to me at checkout number eighteen and stare at each item as I packed them in the bags. I smiled at him and nodded my head in acknowledgement, but nothing came back. In fact, he just moved even closer, his head almost burrowing into my basket of shopping. I continued packing in silence, like a prisoner changing clothes in front of a guard. It felt like my privacy was being invaded, such was the intensity of the scrutiny. With this sort of thing happening each time I went to the supermarket, suddenly I could take no more.

'Why don't you just bugger off?' I enquired.

He regarded me without a flicker of emotion.

'I said, why don't you just bugger off!'

Still nothing. With my anger rising, I inexplicably found myself raising a baguette in his general direction. What was I going to do? Beat him to death with a piece of French bread? I don't think so. Either way, that was the excuse he needed. To the bemusement of the checkout girl, and despite my protestations, he confiscated the baguette and the rest of the shopping and marched me outside. He then stood there at the entrance, baguette still in hand, making sure I would not attempt to sneak back in.

Another time I was in a shop called Sedmoy Kontinent, or in English, 'Seventh Continent' – Moscow's attempt at an upmarket food department store, but without the class or service to back up the claims. Disconcertingly, I had on occasion discovered fish and meat on the shelves that appeared to be past the sell-by date, not uncommon in the Russian supermarkets that I had been to. Nonetheless, it was expensive, so naturally this is where you would find Moscow's elite at play. Or really, I should say the *wives* of Moscow's elite at play. Rich Russian men hardly ever did the shopping, whereas their fur-clad wives (or mistresses) were quite happy to do so; it was a chance to show everyone how privileged they were. It's what we in Britain call 'new money'. People who have suddenly become rich for whatever reason and think that in order to prove themselves they have to show off to all and sundry how cool and loaded they are. Pathetic really, but it's the same the world over, isn't it? In Britain, 'new money' goes out and buys Bentley cars and racehorses. In Moscow they go shopping at Sedmoy Kontinent wearing their best Chanel, high heels and gaudy gold jewellery. You can tell I didn't like this store, but it was close to where I lived, so was regrettably convenient. Anyway, one day I was at the checkout with a basketful of food. You know how sometimes the checkout person seems to be able to 'bleep' and throw the food down towards you with incredible speed? Well, this girl was doing it with superhuman agility.

Bleep, throw! Bleep, throw! Bleep, throw! As a result, I was not quite able to keep up, as vegetables, tins of beans, cartons of juice and slices of cheese all flew my way in a flurry of mixed up food and plastic bags. As I struggled to put everything in the various bags, I noticed a tall, well-dressed middle-aged Russian woman with what looked like two dead foxes wrapped around her neck, waiting impatiently in the queue behind me.

'Hurry up!' she barked.

I looked up. Was she talking to me?

'Hurry up!' she repeated.

'I'm doing my best.'

There then followed a most unexpected response.

'You black monkey! Know your place!'

My initial reaction should have been deep offence, though strangely enough I was just intrigued and somewhat amused. However, my laughter simply infuriated her more.

'Get back to Africa! Get back to Africa!'

I regarded this woman with interest. And as her tirade continued, my mirth wore thin and I considered throwing a packet of cheese slices at her (first the baguette incident, now cheese. Where would it all end?). Resisting that urge, I decided instead to give her some of her own verbal medicine. I would love to tell you about the sophisticated and intelligent responses I gave her – so intelligent in fact that it stopped her in her tracks and reduced her to the size of an intellectual pygmy. But alas, that wouldn't be the truth.

'You stupid, ugly, sour-faced cow,' I replied, surprising myself at what I had been driven to say out loud in the middle of a busy supermarket. Moscow was certainly leading me to do things I never knew I had in me. She went mental.

'You black monkey!' she repeated, shaking with fury. 'Get out of Moscow! Get out of Moscow!'

The other shoppers were regarding this altercation with bemused interest, while the security guards came over and watched, but seemed unable to comprehend what was going on. A whole dictionary of insults followed, as we traded increasingly graphic smears and allegations. Finally, I headed to the exit, throwing one last insult over my shoulder, before walking out into the cold. Outside, I walked a short way and then stopped for a moment to pause for reflection. I was actually shaking a little and realised that the incident had affected me more than I had thought. It's one thing to be involved in a stand-up row with a stranger in a country you know, but doing so in a place you don't is that much more unsettling, as you have no idea where the parameters are and what would have happened if violence had ensued. I mean, I doubt I would have resorted to throwing slices of cheese at her, but you never know how these things will end up and you always wish you'd said something cleverer in these circumstances, but that's life.

As I looked around at the sea of Russian faces around me in the street, I suddenly felt a pang of homesickness for Britain. A good pint in a traditional pub with friendly staff who spoke English, followed by fish and chips on the way home and a night in watching *Strictly Come Dancing* on telly. English-speaking satellite TV had not made it to most apartments in Moscow; you had to be rich or connected to get around that one. There were no cheap Indian or Chinese takeaways. No fresh British sausages, no Bisto gravy granules, no custard. Some imported stuff was available of course, but it cost a fortune. A small bottle of ketchup, for example, was the equivalent of around seven quid. Yet who was I to complain? Before the 1990s, people here felt lucky to get any food at all, let alone brand names and instant gravy. I looked down at the bags of shopping I had put down on the snowy ground. It had been my first brush with any kind of hostility in Moscow and would serve to sharpen my senses for the rest of my time here. I gathered up my shopping and moved on.

Racism was certainly an issue in Moscow. There was definitely a strata of young Russian adult males in particular who were deeply nationalist, bordering on fascist. Much of this manifested itself around football, with fans of certain teams nurturing aggression not just against other teams, but also against non-Russians outside the sport. There were said to be a good few hundred African students studying in various Moscow universities, yet I hardly ever saw any of them in the streets and definitely not on the Metro. The Metro was where any trouble was most likely to take place and most of those students felt deeply threatened by the hostility that many of them had experienced. A good number had been verbally and physically abused. Yet the connection between Russia and African countries went back decades, when the former Soviet Union was attempting to consolidate its influence in different parts of the world, especially during the Cold War. Many African countries were courted and feted in an attempt to woo them away from any possible influence from the United States, and although the strategic importance of many of those countries had waned over the years as far as Russia was concerned, the legacy of that period was everywhere to be seen in Moscow in the form of huge and extraordinarily ornate embassy buildings, most of which seemed to be standing empty. Zambia, Tanzania, Cameroon, Mozambique, Kenya... they all had diplomatic buildings, each of which took up half a block in very prestigious areas, with the various national flags of every nation hanging outside – sometimes the flag itself would be ripped and muddied through years of neglect. I had heard a story of one African couple living in Moscow who had very poorly paid cleaning jobs and were often out of work, but were nonetheless allowed to reside in one of the residential wings of their country's embassy, due to a diplomatic agreement. In effect, they lived in absolute luxury and complete poverty all at the same time.

Anyway, the young racist thugs occasionally held public rallies to advance their insidious views. Once, thousands had gathered very close to Red Square, chanting slogans and issuing Nazi salutes. Strange to see Nazi salutes in a country which suffered so much at the hands of Hitler's war machine. Yet here they all were, with hate in their eyes and vitriol on their lips, complaining about the presence of *any* foreigner, no matter what colour they were. Worryingly, those in government seemed content to tolerate this, blaming foreigners for the country's woes – small-minded ministers deflecting attention away from their own ministerial incompetence, in a naked bid to win votes. At one point they decided to 'clear out' people who had arrived from other parts of Russia to find work in Moscow. 'They are taking our jobs,' they reasoned. These were people who had Russian passports but basically had darker skin. It's like saying that anyone from Manchester who arrives in London and has black hair instead of blonde has to leave because 'They are taking our jobs.' Ridiculous. Though not everyone in Russia is racist of course. To say so would be racist in itself. Normal-thinking Russians did exist; they just seemed that much harder to find.

There was also a growing tension between nationalist thugs and young migrant workers from Central Asia and the Caucasus. In times of economic crisis, it's the migrants who get the blame for everything when things go wrong, especially when it comes to unemployment. Yet, it was they who did all the badly paid 'dirty' jobs, in poor working conditions with very few rights; jobs that the protestors would turn their noses up at. The street cleaners, the hotel workers, the people who toiled in silent acknowledgement that their lives would not get any better, yet were still doing their best to raise families with the few opportunities they had in the hope that their children might see a more prosperous future. It's a cruel world. And that cruelty was soon to manifest itself in one shocking and violent moment.

March would see the arrival of Saint Patrick's Day, celebrated by Irish people across the world and anyone else who likes to party. The snow and ice of winter had largely melted, making way for street processions through the centre of town. There was, like any other city, an Irish contingent living and working in Moscow, though interestingly the Russians had adopted Paddy's Day with gusto – dressing up in oversized green leprechaun hats, painting their faces with the Irish tricolour and downing as many pints of stout as their constitutions would allow, which for Russians is quite a lot. It was certainly a colourful and noisy street carnival and I surmised that Russians liked to party, given any excuse to do so. For countless years they had been so stifled of the chance to express themselves that to have unbridled fun must have been a liberating experience indeed. The sun was shining for the first time in months and the atmosphere in Moscow had lightened as people looked forward to spring and the chance to walk along a pavement without constantly worrying about slipping on the ice and breaking their bones. And that atmosphere continued over the next few days. Until a bomb went off in the Metro.

In previous years as a reporter in the UK, I had covered many events of a violent nature. Take the Paddington rail crash in London in 1999, for example. Thirty-one people were killed when two commuter trains hit each other on the same track coming into London. I was sent to do some initial reports for the BBC, and I remember standing by the track looking at the mangled wreckage, already writing my report in my head:

'It was just after 8am this morning when a high-speed passenger train arriving into London collided with another train leaving Paddington. We're not quite sure of all the details yet, but we understand there are many casualties. Witnesses say they heard a loud bang and...'

You just go into autopilot, because that's what you are trained for; if you spent all day worrying about the horror of it all, you would never actually do a report. But just occasionally, something would happen which would supersede your professional detachment. A whole flock of journalists and broadcast vans bedecked with satellite dishes had arrived by the side of the track, with yapping reporters breathlessly telling the story to the pointing cameras. Every now and then a police officer would beckon the reporters over for an official update and they would bound after him or her like puppies after a ball. Huge cranes and moving equipment had been drafted in to deal with the wreckage of the carriages, while forensic scientists went into the carriages themselves to begin the gruesome work of identifying the bodies. Some families of the victims complained bitterly over why it was taking so long to do this. The answer was difficult to comprehend. A fireball had almost completely destroyed one of the carriages as the fuel from the diesel had ignited on impact, so the reason it had been so difficult to identify the bodies was because in many cases, there was simply nothing left to identify. Who, as a human being, would be able to explain that to a grieving relative?

Then at night there would be an eerie scene, as specially rigged spotlights with their own electric generators were erected over the wreckage, allowing the authorities to continue their work. Because night had fallen, it was much quieter and the police had cordoned off much of the area to prevent curious (or just morbid) members of the public from approaching. As I stood there shivering in the cold, I heard someone's mobile phone ringing, but it didn't belong to a reporter. A second phone began to ring, but again no one was answering. It was then that I realised the phones were coming not from the side of the track, but from within one of the mangled carriages that had been flung off the line. Inside, the white-suited forensic experts were slowly walking around, casting odd shadows with their alien-like outfits. But the mobile phones that were ringing did not belong to them either. They belonged to some of those who had not survived the accident. Relatives and friends who had reported them missing, but had not yet received confirmation of their deaths, frantically calling their loved ones to find out if they were safe. The forensics had been instructed not to answer. What could they say? The phones rang and rang inside the carriages until the batteries were exhausted, and then they fell silent. That was the moment that affected me most. That awful silence when you realised that a relative on the other end had not received the answer they had prayed for. I called it my 'Paddington moment'. It had left a lasting impact on me. Several years later those memories and feelings were to rise to the surface again, this time in

Moscow. I was on shift presenting the news in the studio and all seemed fine. A few political stories, followed by a world news round-up, followed by the business bulletin. Nothing out of the ordinary.

'Cary, we have some breaking news you need to announce,' said the producer in my earpiece speaker.

'Oh really? What do we have?'

'We think there's been a bomb on the Metro at Park Kultury station.'

Oh my God, I thought. That Metro station was just a minute's walk away from the studio and at that time of the morning it would have been packed with commuters.

'Okay, let's do it.'

Suddenly, the newsroom went into action mode – shouting, pointing, phones going off, reporters deployed, instructions going back and forth, stressed faces and frantic fingers over keyboards. Gradually, other TV networks from around the world began to tune in to what was happening.

CNN: 'We have some breaking news from Russia now...'

BBC: 'We are getting reports of an explosion on the Moscow Metro...'

Al Jazeera: 'Some news just in from Russia...'

It transpired that a teenage widow, whose husband had been killed by Russian forces in the Caucasus, had blown herself up on the Metro platform, leaving carnage and devastation in her wake. For a few hours, Moscow, and indeed my own news programme, was at the centre of the world. It was a non-stop studio shift, without time to eat, drink, or even go to the toilet. I was definitely in autopilot mode. Studio guests came and went and live interviews were done with correspondents at the scene. Footage of the aftermath of the incidents (there had also been another explosion at Lubyanka station) had been filmed on people's mobile phones, showing body parts all over the platform, smoke, and panicked passengers rushing for the exits. The advent of new technology makes everyone a news reporter and the internet means images now shoot around the world like lightning strikes. So far nothing had really registered with me in terms of feeling emotional about it; I was just too busy working. But like my 'Paddington moment' there was to be a 'Moscow moment' too, when the reality of what had happened broke down my defensive barriers.

'Cary, Yulia's coming into the studio.'

Yulia Shapovalova was a fellow presenter – a tall, good-natured Russian woman. She was professional, knowledgeable and excellent at her job. She was also an all-round nice person. But why was she coming into the studio? After all, she had just finished her presenting shift before me. What on earth was going on?

'Yulia was down the Metro when it went off; she's coming back in to tell us what happened,' the producer informed me.

The door to the studio with the red 'On Air' light above it opened up and in came an ashen-faced Yulia. A normally calm and composed individual, she was clearly still in shock. I wondered whether she would get through the broadcast. I had about thirty seconds to talk to her before we went live on air. She sat down next to me, a haunted expression on her face as she hurriedly attached her microphone lead and tried to focus. Unable to steady her shaking fingers, her microphone wire became draped untidily over her shoulder and down her front. Normally, a studio assistant would tidy it out of the way, but right now it didn't seem to matter, and anyway there wasn't time – we had just a few seconds left.

'You'll be fine. When we go on air, just tell me slowly what happened, okay?' I whispered in her ear. She nodded. The 'On Air' light came on, so I began…

'We can talk now to Yulia Shapovalova here in the studio… Yulia, you actually left the RT studios here and walked down to Park Kultury Metro station where one of these blasts occurred… what happened?'

For a moment her head was bowed and I wondered if she was going to say anything at all. Then she looked up. Part of what she said went like this:

'That's right, as you say I had just finished my shift, and er… and er… was going home… and er…'

She put her hand to her temple, paused, and took a deep breath.

'… and as soon as I got downstairs I saw two Metro trains…'

The tears were welling up in her eyes, her throat was getting choked up and she was shaking, but she persevered.

'… I personally saw a young woman covered with blood, and another was so scared so she was crying, the third one was talking to someone by her mobile phone thanking God for her survival, and after all that I started realising that I had survived myself, so I consider myself very lucky indeed… I had heard the blast itself…'

Her account continued in this vein. It's only when you hear it from someone who was actually there that you start to glimpse the moment. And for a while, her graphic recollections gripped the world, as rival TV stations all tuned in to watch our coverage.

'Okay, we'll leave it there for now, RT's Yulia Shapovalova, thank you very much for coming in and sharing with us your thoughts.'

As I write this, that very broadcast is still on YouTube for all to see.

We went to another recorded report which gave us a minute to allow Yulia to leave the studio.

'Hey, well done,' I said.

'Thanks,' she replied, before walking unsteadily out.

It then dawned on me that many of my colleagues would have been using that Metro station to come to work. Fortunately, no one I knew was caught up in the tragedy, but many colleagues had friends who were injured and even killed. The rest of my shift continued until, exhausted, I handed over the reins to another presenter. Professionally, I had proven myself to my new employers, as the programme had been as accomplished as it could have been in the circumstances. Though at that moment, it seemed of little consequence if I got a pat on the back or not. Only after I had finished did the full drama of what I had been presenting to the world finally get through to me. Throughout history, the often unreported and unseen reality of the bombing and killing of innocent civilians – whether by out of control Russian-backed militia in Chechnya, wayward so-called 'precision' bombs by the U.S. military in Iraq, or just an extremist with an explosive strapped to the chest – all results in the same thing. Limbs, internal organs and brains spattered all over the place. Many will die instantly, while others will suffer unimaginable pain as they bleed to death looking at their own dismembered limbs, with many more maimed for life. TV reports somehow manage to sanitise it, with commentaries that make the unpalatable slightly more palatable.

'Ten people were killed in a roadside bombing this morning…' say the newscasts, without giving graphic details of exactly what that means.

'There was an Israeli incursion into territory controlled by…' say the reports. 'Incursion'. As if the army went over the border for a couple of hours, popped out of their tanks, had a picnic, and came back. No gory details of the innocents slaughtered along the way. We have become detached and immune to it all and in some ways perhaps we don't really want to know. Too horrible to contemplate and too dreadful to discuss, as we tuck into our breakfast cornflakes and guiltily change the channel.

The aftermath of the Moscow Metro bombings saw a visible increase in security personnel on the streets of the city and a general beefing-up of security everywhere. In true Russian dogged style, the Metro was up and running again in no time and for a while impromptu memorials appeared where the bombings had taken place. People had propped up framed photos of their dead relatives on tables and laid flowers all around, right there on the platforms. Gradually, more and more people laid flowers, until the middle of the platforms had become unofficial shrines, with candles, wreaths and personal mementos. It did not need to be officially organised or protected. It was as though there was an invisible force field encircling the shrines which meant there was a respectful space in front, while members of the travelling public ringed around it, each pausing for a few minutes in contemplation. Every now and then someone would puncture the imaginary force field to walk up and lay a wreath of flowers, before backing away slowly. It was a tense and poignant scene; a strange oasis of silence within a platform of noisy Metro trains and the bustling sounds of thousands of commuters. After a week or so, the authorities came and carefully removed the wreaths and candles, and life carried on as normal, albeit with repercussions. Some of my expat co-workers suffered violent attacks in subways, leaving two male colleagues in hospital. The attackers wanted retribution against anyone non-Russian and weren't content with just taking wallets; they also wanted to inflict physical harm. Threats and all manner of vile rantings were rife across chat rooms and social media. Our general coverage of the bombings had been uploaded to YouTube. Out of interest, I took a look to see what my professional performance had been like. Underneath the first video of me introducing the 'breaking news', people had posted various opinions about the blasts and what should be done about it. The first comment, however, was directed at me.

'Nigger, get out of Moscow,' it said.

I didn't read the rest.

That night, I went out for a few beers with some friends to a local bar. There were less people out and about than usual, probably a human reaction to an event such as the bombing – people weren't really in the mood to move on yet; they just wanted to play it safe for a while. At the end of the evening, and rather drunk, I decided to walk home alone. Normally, this wasn't an issue in the central area where most of us expats were based. Tonight though, I sensed a tension. The streets seemed colder and more menacing than usual, because the normally populated pavements and underpasses were largely empty. Not that Moscow was the sort of place where anyone would come to your aid if you were being assaulted, but still I felt even less comfortable than usual traversing all the empty concrete boulevards in the near darkness of a freezing unfriendly night. Too late now though. I looked at my watch. 11.40pm. I hurried on, taking the steps down into an underpass which could not be avoided, given that it was the only way to cross the highway to the zone where my apartment block was situated. Once at the bottom of the steps I looked at the route ahead – an empty, dark, concrete tunnel, with no people whatsoever. I started walking. Halfway through, I turned to look over my shoulder. Still no one. I looked ahead at the remaining half and involuntarily started running. Finally, I got to the other side, ran up the steps to the open street and paused to catch my breath. Phew. My head was dizzy from the running, and from the beer that I had definitely had one too many of. I tried to focus on the task in hand. My apartment was probably only a ten-minute walk away now, down this straight boulevard and a little to the left. I started walking, cold breath streaming from my lips, thinking about the invitingly warm and safe apartment that was waiting for me. I passed two young guys leaning against a lamp post, their faces wrapped up with scarves against the biting cold. They didn't look at me, but just stood hunched under the dim glow of the street lamp. I hurried on, trying to focus on walking in a straight line, while also avoiding the worst of the ice on the frozen pavement. And then... I sensed something. That primeval feeling you get when the hairs start to rise on the back of your neck, and you know someone or something is watching you. It's an awareness which cannot be explained by science – you just *know* you are being hunted. I stopped and turned around, and there they were again, the same scarf-faced guys hunched under a lamp post. Except I had walked a good two hundred metres, and this was a different lamp post. They were following me. I turned and walked on, a little faster this time, my senses heightened, the alcohol in my blood seemingly replaced by adrenalin. Suddenly, I could hear the 'crunch' of every footstep I was making, mirrored by the footsteps of my uninvited stalkers. Were they getting nearer? Yes. I walked a little faster again, and sure enough, the 'crunches' behind me matched my speed. This was no time for misplaced bravado. I ran, with the two men in hot pursuit. When you are running for your life, it's amazing how much energy your body can find and direct to your legs. You wonder where all this energy was when you were competing and failing in school athletics days. Something superhuman overcomes you. I'd heard stories of people who had been involved in car accidents, who were inexplicably able to lift impossibly heavy parts of the wreckage off injured loved ones. In the heat of a crisis, we as humans can perform stunning feats, which in normal circumstances are beyond us. Plus, the threat here in the streets of Moscow was no fanciful imagining on my part. One of my Arabic work colleagues had one night been attacked and beaten by a gang of knife-wielding Russians in a subway not far from the office, his pleas for help ignored by all and sundry. His injuries were so severe he was eventually flown back for treatment in his home country. He never returned.

As I neared my apartment, I began to retrieve my front door keys from my pocket. Some money fell to the floor as I did so, but I ignored it and ran on, feeling the burning pain in my chest as my lungs struggled to keep up with my continuing desire for oxygen. I had not looked back once since beginning to run, fearing losing my footing and losing even a split second of my head start. The communal door to my block was now in sight and I headed towards it like a man possessed. I thrust the key into the door lock – the first time I had managed it on the first attempt. Normally, I would fish out the wrong key, or try to put it in upside down. But this time, with the focus of a chased man, there was no mistake. Were my pursuers still behind me? At this point, I honestly didn't know. The instinct for survival had taken over. Door open, going in, door slammed shut behind. Run up stairs (not waiting for lift).

Key out. Into apartment. Door shut. Look through spy-hole. No one. Collapse on sofa. Chest rising and falling rapidly. Hands shaking. Clothes covered in sweat. But safe.

I caught my breath, paused for a while longer, then made myself a cup of tea and sat contemplating – a single small lamp casting dark shadows around the living room. What a night. In fact, what a month. It had been eventful to say the least – full of tension and darkness. I hoped I wouldn't experience another one like it. As it turned out, the following period would thankfully be a time of healing – Russian style.

4

SAUNAS, SPEED DATING, AND SPIES

'I was to strip naked before pouring myself a cup of tea'

Russians have a love affair with saunas. I'm not sure where this love comes from though. I suppose the obvious answer is that when you are living in a country that's so amazingly cold in winter, you tend to go to the opposite extreme to keep warm. But that's just a guess. Either way, I had been curious for some time to experience what was known as the Russian *banya* – essentially a great big sauna, but with some very Russian rituals thrown in for good measure. I had read about some large and very posh marble *banyas* in the centre of Moscow, frequented by the rich and famous, full of stunning marble statues and Romanesque mosaic designs. The tourist books are full of them, extolling the virtues of the history of the buildings etc. But that was the exact opposite of what I wanted to do. I wanted to see where the 'ordinary' Russians went, not the tourists. As such, I was advised by a Russian work colleague to visit one on the edge of the city, in an area regarded as being a bit rough, but that's what getting the most from living in a foreign country is all about – exploration.

So off I went on the Metro to the outer suburbs of Moscow. On exiting the station, I got a bit of a shock, for up until then I had only really seen the centre of town, and the suburbs were not pretty. I was confronted by a landscape of tall, ugly, grey concrete apartment blocks where people lived like battery hens. If you got a set of dominoes, painted them grey and then stood them up in a line on a concrete pavement in front of you, then you would just have created a mini version of what I was seeing in front of me. Hideous. I had been told that Moscow was not atypical of Russia and that the majority of Russians in the rest of the country lived a very different and much poorer life. Well, if the suburbs of the city were anything to go by, I was in for an even bigger shock if I ever went any further afield. This is what was going on in the Soviet Union when no one else was looking, or even cared. Mass, rushed housing construction, erected as cheaply and inelegantly as possible. And this was still part of the capital. Anyway, I wasn't there to dissect the architecture, I was there to find a Russian sauna. A look at my trusty and creased street map revealed that the *banya* should be about a hundred metres down the street on the left. When I got to where it should have been, there was just a grey metallic doorway, more akin to a prison than a place of relaxation. By this time, however, I had become accustomed to plain doorways actually being the gateways to the most unusual of experiences, so I went ahead and rang the intercom. A crackly Russian voice came back, to which I could not reply (when was I going to learn how to speak this impenetrable language?).

'Er… can I come in?'

Silence.

'Hello?' I persisted.

More silence. How was this going to work?

'Hello, I wonder if…'

The door buzzed open and I was in. I was met by a dull green interior with faded and peeling brown wallpaper and two people sitting at a heavy wooden table – a middle-aged man and a woman. They regarded me with incredulity, but not unfriendliness. They were probably as curious about me as I was about them. What on earth was this tourist doing so far off the beaten track?

'How… do… I… use… the… *banya*?' I asked, in an embarrassingly 'I am British, I will speak very sloooowly so you can understand' kind of way. They smiled and pointed towards a window which housed yet another receptionist. I went over and looked at her and she just looked back and nothing happened – a very Russian situation. And then I spied an old cash register complete with knobs and levers and deduced that this must be the payment area. I handed over some roubles and was given a small ticket, before returning to the two behind the table, wondering why it had taken a third person to take my money. This, I supposed, was job creation. Without bureaucracy and paperwork, half of Russia would be unemployed. They smiled again and gestured to two separate corridors. This was going to be an exercise in hand signals, but by observing the other visitors, I saw that one corridor was for men and the other for women – a strictly segregated pastime. The corridor I chose opened out into a kind of locker room where I was met by two ageing men, one next to some white towels, the other next to a table of fruit tea and biscuits. More hand signals followed as I slowly got the idea that I was to strip naked, before pouring myself a cup of tea. The other guys around me seemed completely unconcerned about their nakedness, not bothering to hide their dangly bits with the small towels provided. With hot tea in one hand, biscuits in the other and a towel wrapped around my privates (I was still not quite ready to bare all) I ventured into the area beyond the locker room, which turned out to be some kind of communal bathing and shower hall. Naked, big-bellied Russian men were chatting loudly to each other, splashing water into ceramic bowls and lumbering through to yet another area, like a group of contented sea lion bulls. The whole place was a labyrinth of marble-tiled washrooms, but where was the actual sauna?

A large Russian man, with a belly the size of a hippo, gave me a gold-toothed grin and a little shove forward. He and a few other Russians were leisurely flip-flopping their way towards a wooden door next to what looked like a cold plunge pool. Next to the pool were several wooden containers containing heaps of dry tree branches with leaves still attached. They each collected a few of these branches and gestured for me to do the same. What on earth was this for? In some confusion I declined the offer of tree branches, at which point one of them swung open the wooden door and a blast of searing heat smacked me square in the face. He continued to motion me forward and we all walked inside. It looked like any other Swedish sauna, though rather larger, with end-to-end wooden-slatted floors and a great big steel contraption in one corner. Three of them unfurled their towels on the floor and proceeded to lie on their backs, while the other one went over to the steel oven thing. The heat was almost overpowering, yet none of them seemed to notice as they sweated buckets onto their soon sopping wet towels. Then, as if it was some kind of reality TV endurance game, the guy by the steel oven started turning iron levers, which started to make the room even hotter! The thing he was fiddling with seemed to be the end product of some kind of industrial underground boiler room. Either that or it was actually the central heating system used to fire up hell itself.

I looked around me. The guys were talking and gesturing to each other, as if this was the place to sort out all of life's concerns, in a male bonding session designed to weed out the men from the boys. And wow, was I starting to feel like one of the boys. Then the whipping started. It turned out that the tree branches were in fact large sprigs of birch, which they were using to whip each other with. I mean, they weren't drawing blood or anything, but elsewhere in the world this could be regarded as a bit painful at best, and decidedly kinky at worst.

Swish! Swish! Swish!

Apparently, it was something to do with the opening up and cleansing of the sweat glands, pores and circulation system. To me though, it looked suspiciously like grown men whipping each other.

Swish! Swish! Swish!

I, however, declined to be whipped, though in true British style I had brought my cup of tea into the sauna with me and as I reached for it, they all stopped talking (and whipping) for a moment and regarded this weird foreigner. I picked up the cup and immediately wished I hadn't.

'Ow!' I yelped in pain, spilling tea all over the floor. The ceramic cup had become red hot as it had heated up in the sauna. They chuckled and went back to their whipping. Meanwhile, the heat was seriously starting to suffocate me, but then I thought, 'I'll show them I'm as tough as they are! I can handle the heat!' Another glance in their direction ten minutes later though and still they were not flinching. How could they take it? Bravado be damned, I had to get out of there. I grabbed my towel, stood up and headed for the door as slowly as I could, so as not to appear that I had been defeated. They saw through this of course, and all started laughing, not in an antagonistic way, but taking the mickey nonetheless. I had lost all of my tea, most of my dignity and an awful lot of fluid, but I was safely out. Don't ever challenge a Russian to a drinking game, or to a 'Who can stay in the sauna longest?' game. Trust me, you will not win.

Then, as if to finish off my *banya* experience with a dose of cultural masochism, I jumped – as instructed by the helpful tea and biscuits attendant – straight into a freezing cold plunge pool that was next to the sauna. That was, after all, what the tourist books said you were supposed to do. I will never read them again. I climbed straight out, shaking. The contrast between the very, very hot and the very, very cold is like a rapid injection of adrenalin. All your senses are suddenly heightened and you feel a strange sense of burning clarity. It also makes you shake uncontrollably. Time for a sit down and another attempt at sipping a new cup of tea. My shaking hands were making the cup clink with the saucer. It must have been a full twenty minutes before the Russians came out of the sauna, their fat sweating tummies proudly thrust before them as they sauntered their way towards the showers. One of them nodded his head at me and I nodded back, a faint smile of relief on my lips. I had survived a Russian rite of passage.

Back on the street, I had to say that I did indeed feel better for visiting the *banya*; cleansed and clear-headed, ready for whatever else Moscow could throw my way. Russians seemed fond of open-air public swimming pools, and even in the middle of winter, Orthodox Church followers had a thing about jumping into icy waters, believing it would cleanse their souls. Certainly, I now felt invigorated and inspired to embark on a healthier lifestyle, so decided to join a gym. I had made this mistake once before in my life though – that of joining a posh gym which I never ever used. I think the *idea* of joining is what I liked best and the fact I could then tell everyone I'd joined a health club and convince myself I was fit and well, simply by popping along every once in a while and ordering a glass of carrot juice. Silly really, and I'm sure the staff could see me coming a mile away, 'Off-peak or full membership, sir?' they would ask, as the sight of their perfectly toned track-suited bodies made me think that I too could look like that in a couple of weeks. And then there are the classes. The yoga classes, the Pilates, the spinning. People go because they either want to look like the instructor, or they just *fancy* the instructor, male or female. And don't tell me it isn't so; I have a friend in North London who's a member of a well-known health club chain. She told me that the flirting and shagging that goes on in these places is amazing, bordering on cult-like. So what would a Russian health club be like? Well, expensive for starters. But on the recommendation of a British colleague and friend named Peter, I joined one within a reputable five-star hotel. By all accounts, Peter was a sporty, good-looking, blue-eyed bloke from Kettering who did some serious workouts in his spare time and certainly hadn't joined the gym just to flash around his membership card at parties. He knew his bench presses from his squat thrusts and had something of a six-pack to prove it. My flabby midriff was starting to get on my nerves, so I decided to improve my ailing physical appearance while indulging in a bit of male bonding. So on a month's trial and, as I say, at some expense, I signed up to the health complex in the Lotte Hotel, in the centre of town.

'I'm not sure I can justify the cost of this,' I lamented to Peter.

He replied, 'If you live all your life like that, you will never justify anything.'

Well, I liked the sound of that mantra, so decided to treat myself to a bit of luxury. Why not?

The hotel itself was as plush as plush can be, with marble floors, enormous chandeliers, gold statues and red carpets. Russians know how to do things to excess. I'm not saying it was stylish, but excessive? Oh yes. In fact, the cost of one night in the all-singing, all-dancing rock star suite would set you back... well... you can imagine. Any thoughts of enticing some lovely Russian goddess from the gym straight up to a room were well and truly dispelled from my mind. I was nowhere near that league.

Anyway, it was down two flights of carpeted stairs to the health club. The gym was equipped with shiny new exercise machines (none of which I knew how to use), a steam room and treatment centre, a swimming pool complete with a twinkling simulated star field on the ceiling, constantly shifting mood lights all around, and that phoney Japanese tea house music that all health clubs seem so fond of, and of course a lot of beautiful women honing and toning their already perfect bodies. All of this was great, until I tried to turn on the poolside Jacuzzi. The 'on' button was simply nowhere to be found. And not being a regular in five-star hotel gyms, I went to the reception desk to ask what to do.

'Okay, no problem, we will send someone.'

It was a full half-hour before anyone arrived and when

they did, they came as a trio – three guys in blue jumpsuits, all of whom completely ignored me. Two of them disappeared to a boiler room round the back and down some stairs, while the other started inspecting the Jacuzzi. First, he put a thermometer in the still water then he fished out an old walkie-talkie from his capacious pockets and began talking away in Russian, presumably to the other guys who were by now busy cranking levers somewhere in the basement. This dunking the thermometer and then saying something into the crackly walkie-talkie routine went on for a further twenty minutes, until suddenly the Jacuzzi started frothing away. Without a word, he deposited his thermometer in his pocket and disappeared. Gingerly I went to inspect the bubbling Jacuzzi. It looked great, so I jumped in. It was freezing. The two boiler room guys appeared from round the corner. One of them stopped for a moment.

'Is okay?'

'Yes, thanks,' I said meekly. Why do we British always say things are great, when patently they are not? It turned out that the reason for all this faffing about was that when the Jacuzzi had been put in, they forgot to install a poolside 'on' button next to it, and because no one wanted to take the responsibility of making the decision to install one without permission, it just never happened. Russians only do what the boss tells them to do and nothing more. If that subsequently results in a whole circuitous way of having to deal with a problem on a daily basis, then that is what they would do, regardless of how absurd it might seem. Go down to the basement and wrestle with a load of levers in the dark in order to turn on the Jacuzzi every time someone wanted to use it? You bet.

It's believed (though historians argue) that when the first Tsar of Russia decided to have a railway built between Moscow and St. Petersburg for their fleet of steam locomotives, he became exasperated with his officials arguing over what route the line should take, given the existence of villages, hills and various landmarks in the way. So he simply got out a ruler and marker and just drew a straight line between the two cities on a map and said sarcastically, 'Like that.' However, he had inadvertently drawn around the finger that he was holding the ruler with. This meant that there was a 'kink' in his line, but so terrified were his minions about arguing with the Tsar, that they ordered the line be built on the exact route that he'd shown them, kink and all. Hence, the construction of an inexplicable seventeen-kilometre semi-circle diversion of track, which still exists to this very day (but more of Russian train journeys later).

Back to my health club, where another oddity was the constantly broken steam room. There was a sign on the opaque entrance door saying 'out of order'. It did actually work, but the ceiling had been painted with the wrong kind of paint. As a result, every time it was switched on, the steam would cause the caustic paint to start peeling off and drip down onto the sweating humans sitting below. But in order to redo the paintwork, the installers wanted to send independent inspectors to observe the problem first hand. But the health club owners would not allow this, frightened they would be sued by someone if the inspectors wrote a report saying that it was indeed dangerous. The result? It never got switched on and it never got fixed. This was how things worked (or didn't work) in Russia. Though occasionally a stoical attitude to life was actually an advantage, as long as authority wasn't involved. In those instances, Russians had a real sense of, 'Let's just get on with it and stop moaning' practicality about them. Take my friend Charlie. He had lived in Moscow for four years and was quite possibly one of the funniest guys I'd ever met. He had mischievous eyes, wispy reddish-brown hair, gold-rimmed glasses and a well-to-do voice – like a kind of wizard's apprentice. He was one of those people who knew how to tell a story, but not in a rehearsed way – it just came out funny. If he told you that his pet dog had just been run over by a car, it would still be funny. He told me a story once, which went something like this:

One day he had done a particularly large slushy poo (his description) in the toilet of his Russian apartment, having eaten something the night before which clearly had not agreed with him. However, when he flushed the loo, the muddy-coloured water and faeces began to slowly *rise* instead of fall, and it looked like it was going to overflow. In a panic, he ran and fetched a plastic bucket and a kitchen soup ladle, crouched down and started quickly ladling the still-rising foul-smelling water out of the toilet and into the bucket, like a demented chef who had just concocted some kind of evil zombie stew. When he had ladled out a good half-bucket of the stinky brew, he carried it to the balcony and left it outside. After all, he couldn't flush it down the toilet, so just decided to deal with it later.

Next, he rang an emergency plumbing company, which turned out to be two Russian guys in overalls, with no equipment. Not even a plunger. What on earth were they going to do? Well, they simply went into the bathroom and without a word, one of them knelt down, rolled up his sleeves and shoved his arm – Wham! – as hard as he could right down the loo and the U-bend. No gloves or anything. Thirty seconds of using himself as a human plunger, he withdrew his arm and held it aloft, excrement dripping down to his armpits, nodding his head, smiling. His colleague flushed the toilet and sure enough the blockage had been dealt with. But the sight and smell was too much for the already unwell Charlie, who immediately retched down the now unblocked loo right in front of them. They laughed and left, clutching their well-earned roubles in their filthy hands. Meanwhile, Charlie later discovered that the undesirable matter he had left on the balcony had frozen solid; it was minus thirty degrees outside after all. So, he had to leave it in the corridor right outside his apartment door to allow it to thaw out, before finally pouring the slushy mixture down the loo, which is where it had come from in the first place. Horrid.

Meanwhile, Peter had told me about three guys he had met in the gym. They all turned out to be professional pilots, whose job it was to ferry rich oligarchs in private planes from one part of Russia to another, or to various swanky locations around Europe. They worked two weeks on, followed by two weeks off, had all their accommodation paid for on a full-time basis at the Lotte Hotel and were paid a fortune for their troubles. When it came to jobs, there really were two different worlds in Moscow – those few who earned unimaginable vats of money, and the majority who earned a pittance. And despite Peter's theory about what was justifiable in life and what wasn't, I decided not to renew my membership at the end of the month, given that I never really used the gym machines at all, thus leaving my ego behind to soak in the frothy waters of the cold Jacuzzi. And as I glanced in awe at the women who were working out on the brand-new treadmills, I decided it was about time I stopped ogling the talent and actually did something about it. I was well and truly ready to undertake the search in earnest for a Russian girlfriend. I already had a hunch where to start looking.

Speed dating is not a new phenomenon in the West. Fifteen or so guys line up opposite fifteen girls and during the course of an evening they all get to meet each other for no longer than three minutes each, as the guys move in rotation from one table to the next. The idea is that you can normally tell within the first three minutes (or less) of meeting someone whether there is going to be a romantic connection or not. I did this in the UK once and it turned out to be quite an enjoyable evening. Meeting fifteen new girls over a couple of glasses of wine, or staying in and watching a miserable soap opera on telly? As Americans would say, 'You do the math.' At the start of the night you get a scorecard, on which you subsequently put ticks or crosses with the pen provided, depending on whether you would like to meet that person again or not. At the end of the evening, the organisers collect the cards and then do the matching up. If you ticked a girl and she also ticked you, then the next day you both receive each other's email addresses, and off you go. If you didn't get a tick from that person, then you wouldn't be sent their details. Simple, safe and elegant.

In the UK, generally the girls do a lot less ticking and are more discerning than the guys, with the men tending to just tick the whole list, in the hope of having sex with anyone. That's men for you. You also find that the guys usually talk too much, in their attempts at impressing the women with how funny they are (or think they are). This is not to say that some women aren't also prone to gabbling. I remember the event I went to in Bristol – this is how my first three-minute date panned out.

Me: 'Hello, I'm Cary…'

Girl: 'Hi, I'm Judith, do you like fishing?'

Me: 'Sorry?'

Judith: 'Fishing, you know, for fish. I love fly fishing, though often people don't realise why it's such a great pastime. I mean, you do have to be organised and make sure you have the right equipment…'

Me: 'Oh, right, so where do you live?'

Judith: '… but it's not just about the kit, it's about how you react to the environment, though at the end of the day there's nothing quite like it when you finally get that tug and…'

And so it went on. And on. And on. You would be amazed how long three minutes can last when your eyes have glazed over. I remember how during the half-time break I went to the toilet and overheard one guy talking to another as they stood there urinating.

'Have you had fisher-woman yet?' the first guy asked.

'Yeah, she's nuts,' replied his mate.

So how would this compare to Russia, where speed dating was a completely new social event? Well, the first company to give it a go came up against an immediate problem – the Russian men refused to rotate. In a man's world like Russia, the men thought it was only natural that they would sit at the tables while the women did the rotating, like some kind of gentleman's club. Gradually, it was explained that this was not a lap dance evening and not a very gentlemanly way of behaving and that the males should do the rotating. That solved, the first speed dating events got off the ground, so I responded to an advert in the English-speaking newspaper *The Moscow News* about future speed dating evenings. It was right next to a section of adverts offering 'massage' services. I hoped it was not going to be some kind of hybrid event like 'speed massage' or something. The mind boggles. In Russia, you never know. Thankfully it turned out to be legitimate. I arrived at the venue, a decent-looking bar-cum-restaurant in the centre of town. I had pondered over what best to wear. If you go in a suit and tie you might look a bit stuffy and up yourself, but if you go in jeans and a T-shirt it looks like you couldn't be bothered to dress up and take no pride in your appearance. As such, I decided to err on the side of smartness, following the maxim that you can always 'dress down' if you look too formal (take off your tie for example) but you can't 'dress up' if you're stuck in casual clothes and haven't brought anything else. So suit it was (with tie in pocket, just in case) with a posh pen in one hand, a glass of red wine in the other, my best watch on my wrist and a pair of silver cufflinks – not gold, because that can make you look ostentatious. Red wine makes you appear more sophisticated than white wine and carrying an expensive pen ensures she doesn't think you're a pauper. I can't remember where I had picked up all these tips and whether women could see straight through them, but I would soon find out.

'Hello, are you here for the speed dating?' enquired the gobsmackingly beautiful blonde Russian organiser, in perfect English.

'Yes, it's Cary.'

She looked down at her list.

'Ah, yes, here you are,' she smiled, while looking up and handing me my name badge and scorecard.

'Thanks,' I replied.

'Just wait in the bar with the other guys; we'll come and get you when we're ready to start. Any questions?'

For a moment, I thought about saying, 'Am I allowed to ask *you* to be my first speed date?' but then thought better of it. Cheesiness can come later in the evening, when I get desperate. I went to the bar as instructed. Now, this is the bit I hated. You have to hang out with a load of blokes at the bar whom you've never met and don't really want to meet (you've come to meet women after all) while making small talk about manly subjects, just in case any passers-by thought you were part of an imaginary gay hook-up of some kind (heterosexual paranoia). And the main subject that men who are strangers feel they can talk to each other about is football. In fact, I think that's why football was invented in the first place – it gives blokes something to converse intensely about any time, any place, without the (misplaced) fear of getting 'too close' to another guy. Ironic really, when you consider that football must have just as many gay people as any other sport, workplace or social gathering.

'Did you see that Messi goal last night?' enquired a large Swedish-sounding guy to my right.

'Naw, I don't really understand soccer,' replied a black American guy to my left. Well, that killed the conversation, didn't it?

Not wanting to talk at all, I moved away from the bar to try and catch a glimpse of the girls who were massing in the adjacent room. The first thing I noticed was that the age difference between the men and the women was a lot wider than at British events. Here at the Moscow speed dating night the girls all appeared to be in their mid-20s, while most of the guys were in their late 30s or 40s. So here we all were. All these Western guys about to meet Russian girls nearly half their age. I used to baulk at stories of men who ended up doing this kind of thing, and yet here it was, happening to me. I had not gone on some kind of paid-for Russian brides excursion, and I had honestly not known what the age range was going to be, yet I still felt like a pervert of some kind. I wondered what my friends back in the UK would say if they could have seen me:

'Cradle-snatcher!'

'Saddo!'

'Sex trafficker!'

I looked down at the name badge pinned to my jacket, my scorecard and favourite pen at the ready in my hand.

'Okay everyone, we're ready to start,' piped up the organiser.

Well, here goes.

Girl 1:   (drop-dead stunner, mousy-haired, bespectacled, quiet voice). I told her my name, my job and why I was in Moscow, while she regarded me with a look of forced interest – like a teacher about to give a pupil a B-minus grade. Don't think she was enthralled.

Girl 2:   (nice-looking, dark-haired, round-faced). Friendly girl, with an air of danger about her, which I rather liked.

'You're the only man who bring own pen,' she remarked with amusement, eyeing my Mont Blanc (I knew that it would count for something!). Our three minutes went by, and I moved on…

Girl 3:   (drop-dead stunner, did not speak any English). Three minutes of unproductive sign language between us.

Girl 4:   (drop-dead stunner, did not speak any English). Three more minutes of unproductive sign language.

Girl 5:   (drop-dead stunner, short jet-black hair in a kind of 'Betty Boop' style). She was called Irina and was from a city called *Rostov-on-Don* in the south of Russia, a place I was to visit later in the year. She was involved in the music industry, though her English was not great so I was a little unsure exactly what it was she did for a living, as I couldn't fully fathom her sentences. She had a look in her eyes which said, 'I know you fancy me, but you'll have to do better than just stare at me though.' For some reason, I couldn't quite get my words out. Probably messed it up.

Girls 6–12: (all drop-dead stunners). No genuine frisson between us, though believe me I would have been delighted to have escorted any of them on my arm.

Girl 13: (drop-dead stunner, tall blonde Barbie doll lookalike). Spent more time looking at the mirror on the wall behind me than actually talking to me.

Girl 14: (drop-dead stunner, long dark hair, big green eyes, gorgeous figure). Her name was Yelena. Intelligent conversation, lots of laughter between us. Could she be the one?!

Girl 15: (what do *you* think?). Can't remember much about her, poor girl, as I was still thinking about Girl 14, or maybe Girl 2.

As the organisers collected our scorecards and I went to collect my coat from the cloakroom, I had a look at the guys I was up against in this battle for the babes. A mixture of British, German and Scandinavian expats, and a couple of Russians too. And there was that American-sounding black guy again, sitting alone at the bar. He glanced in my direction. Strangely, he didn't seem to have taken part in the actual speed dating, and something in his demeanour told me he was not quite what he seemed, which instantly sparked my curiosity.

That was how I met Adeboye.

It turned out that Adeboye was of Nigerian heritage. He was a tall, well-built guy with immaculate clothing, a shaved head, manicured hands and a gravelly American accent. Having spotted him again, I went across to say hello. For those of you who don't know, there is a kind of unofficial 'brotherhood' for black guys, which means that if you are in the middle of nowhere, where there weren't many other black guys, you would always nod your head in recognition of your… well… 'brother' I suppose. It didn't mean you would suddenly be best mates or even buy each other drinks; it just meant you were saying, 'Hey, brother, take it easy, man.' And although we weren't in the middle of nowhere – we were in a big city after all – it was still a city with very few black faces, and that kind of scarcity tends to intensify the feeling of brotherhood. I once had an Irish girlfriend called Colleen, who remarked on this as we walked hand in hand down O'Connell Street in the centre of Dublin. We were passing another couple – a girl of mixed race and a black guy with dreadlocks. As usual, I did my brotherhood nod to him.

'I can't believe you nod to every feckin' black guy we see,' she said incredulously.

But anyway, Adeboye and I started chatting and he told me how he had been thinking about taking part in the speed dating, but was unsure, so decided just to come as a spectator.

Bing! Off went an alarm bell at the back of my mind. This was odd moment number one. He did not strike me as a shy kind of character, so why would he not be confident enough to actually take part?

Adeboye said he worked for a multi-national investment company based in Tokyo, but was evasive about the name.

Bing! Odd moment number two. Anyone who works for a worldwide investment company would probably name the company straight out; if it's famous, he would be proud to be working for them, and for all he knew I could be a potential investor. He then said he was on a three-month attachment and was being put up in the penthouse of the Marriott Hotel for all that time, on company expenses.

Bing! Odd moment number three. Even rich companies draw the line somewhere and I knew that the top floor of the Marriott would cost an absolute fortune for a three-month stay – you would have to be a megastar or at the very least the actual company director to justify that kind of expense, or else be the most successful investment manager that ever lived.

After a couple of drinks, Adeboye said it would be great to meet up again as he was new in town, to which I readily agreed – another partner in crime was fine by me, and I was curious about the things that didn't seem to add up. I gave him my business card, but instead of giving me his, he wrote down his email address and his work mobile phone number on the back of a beer mat, claiming he'd run out of cards.

Bing! Another odd moment to add to my growing list. A man who works for a Japanese company cannot survive for five minutes without a veritable mountain of business cards. As far as I could tell, Japanese business people give each other cards more or less the moment they set eyes on each other. I looked at the email address he'd given me. It wasn't a company one, though that in itself was not necessarily unusual; often people don't want to mix business with pleasure. He did, however, strike me as a fun guy, so I ignored the alarm bells for now and headed home.

The next day I received an email from the speed dating people, revealing three email 'ticks' and contact details, one from Girl 14 Yelena, one from Girl 5 Irina, and one from Girl 2 whose name I had shamefully forgotten, but was reminded in the email that she was called Olga. This always makes you feel good about yourself of course, as it's some kind of proof that you are not a complete ogre – albeit in Moscow, where the women do a lot more ticking than the men, as they continue to search for that elusive single guy. So I ignored the fact that they had also probably ticked half a dozen others. I could, for a short time at least, put myself on some kind of pedestal. Not a very high one, but a pedestal nonetheless. I contacted Yelena and suggested we went out for dinner. It turned out that she was a student at Moscow State University. How old did she tell me she was at the speed dating thing? Don't remember her telling me she was a student. I was starting to feel like a pervert again. I suppose she could be a mature student, so not quite yet time to hand myself over to the police.

She responded to my offer of dinner with a counterproposal. She would agree to come out, but only if she chose the restaurant. This I thought would be fine. The thing about first dates is that you want to impress with somewhere nice, but you also don't want to spend a fortune on someone whom you might not end up liking. It's a fine balance, but as she was a student I thought I would be okay in that department, as she probably didn't frequent very expensive places. So, Yelena and I met outside a Metro station in town and she led me to the venue for our dinner date. As we arrived and she began taking off her winter layers by the cloakroom, I couldn't help noticing that she was a real cracker. Long brown swishy hair, a figure to die for, and huge green eyes, which were even bigger than I remembered. We proceeded into the restaurant and I instantly realised that this was no student haunt. On the contrary, it was as plush and over-the-top as you can imagine, with sumptuous tablecloths, a whole range of spotless wine glasses on each table and waiters who only seemed to have one task each. One to get the food menu, one for the wine, one to rearrange the cutlery, one to pick up crumbs from the floor, one to smile at you, and presumably one to hold your dick in the loo (I hoped not).

When the menus arrived, there were no prices next to the food choices, and that could only mean one thing – if you have to ask, then you can't afford it. As for the wine list, well that *did* have prices, but more akin to what you would expect if you were buying the whole vineyard. Yelena did look fabulous though and we got on quite well. We seemed to be at the best table in the restaurant, perched as it was on the edge of a top floor balcony overlooking the entire place and I wondered how many other unsuspecting Western blokes she had brought here. Or was I being unfair? It seemed that my modest 'student' had taken me to the most expensive Italian restaurant in the whole of Moscow, if not the world, leaving me to mull over my misplaced patronising attitude that assumed she would be a 'cheap' date. Served me right. Needless to say, when the bill eventually arrived, I got stung for an enormous amount, while she smiled and looked me straight in the eye, weighing up in her mind whether I was going to be able to fund this sort of thing on a regular basis. Having decided that the answer was probably 'no' (after I refused the second bottle of massively overpriced Moët) she gave me a hug before trotting off to the Metro, never to be seen again. A seemingly lovely girl, but underneath it all, not quite what she appeared to be.

It was getting late, but for Moscow there is no such thing as 'late' when it comes to socialising. The motto here was, 'Moscow never sleeps' and it was pretty much spot-on. That being the case, and feeling slightly deflated from my date, I rang the mercurial Adeboye. He answered the phone.

'Yeah?' he said, in an offhand manner, while audibly chomping on some food.

Bing! Odd moment number five. As the representative of a large investment company (or so he said) wouldn't you expect him to answer the phone with a fairly formal, 'Hello, Adeboye speaking' rather than a, 'Yeah?' What if I had been a rich client with a huge amount of money to invest?

'It's Cary here.'

'Oh, sure,' he drawled in his gravelly American accent.

'I'm in town, just wondered if you fancied a drink somewhere?'

'Yeah, let's do it.'

We met up at a loud music bar called The Real McCoy, a packed spit and sawdust music joint which never failed to amuse. Full of unpretentious party people and an awful lot of cheap cocktails, served around the legs of girls who had decided that they would rather boogie on the bar than the actual dance floor. Adeboye immediately attracted attention from a tall blonde lady and I felt a pang of jealousy. How had he managed that so quickly? He definitely had an air of mystery about him. He was dancing away with this girl while I sat at a small table in the corner with our drinks. He had forgotten his mobile phone on the table and it started to ring. In the din of the music I picked up the phone, intending to go and hand it to him, but with the pair of them gyrating suggestively, I decided not to interrupt. I sat down again and regarded the still ringing mobile in my hand, which lit up at regular intervals. I looked at the identity of the caller. There was no name, but it was a United States code. As it continued to ring, the flashbacks of odd moments came back to me in a flurry. Here he was, this man with an American accent, with no fixed abode, with no business cards, with a vague unspecified job, with lots of money to spend... I wondered, could Adeboye be... an American spy? I put the phone down and for a fleeting moment thought about using a handkerchief to wipe it down in case my fingerprints would cause me to be implicated in... what exactly? Heck, I could be wrong, maybe he's just an international man of mystery who likes to stay in expensive hotels, bum around the world and keep himself to himself. Like some kind of secret millionaire. Mind you, was he really even staying in a hotel? He said he was in the Marriott, but I remembered that there were several Marriott hotels in Moscow and he had not specified which one – another convenient cover. It's funny, we always think spies will look like caricatures in fictional novels, or that real-life Russian spy Anna Chapman, though of course for covert reasons they probably mostly look very ordinary. I mean if you think about it, 007 always comes into a room looking as conspicuous as possible, sporting a black bow-tie and white dinner jacket, attracting as much attention as he can muster by blowing huge amounts of money on the roulette table – hardly the best way of fitting in and going unnoticed. In reality and by necessity, spies must come in all shapes and sizes, just like people do. Adeboye was black, but that didn't mean he couldn't be a spy too.

I looked at him, flirting away with this girl and wondered how the evening would end up. Should I confront him? Of course not. What you don't know can't hurt you, right? And why did I care anyway? I suppose it was just the buzz of wanting to know something that very few other people knew. That's what gossip is about isn't it? How many times have you gone into work and said to someone, 'Hey, you'll never guess what I've just found out!' It's the satisfaction of being the centre of attention for a short while. It can brighten an otherwise dull working day. But then knowing for sure would put my life at risk, wouldn't it? Of course, I could just have imagined the whole thing and it had simply been his grandmother who happened to live in America calling to wish him happy holidays. But my gut feeling told me that the spy theory may have been right, despite a conspicuous lack of tangible proof. After all, there had to be a few spies *somewhere* in Moscow. The phone finally stopped buzzing and vibrating across the table. Adeboye came back over. He motioned to his dance partner whom he'd left at the bar.

'Sexy girl,' he drawled. 'I got her phone number.'

He picked up his phone and looked at it.

'Oh yes, someone called for you,' I said carefully.

He paused.

'Did ya answer it?' he asked, swigging a bottled beer.

'No, you looked a bit busy.'

'Ah, right.' He shot me a look, but I avoided his gaze.

'So, she going back to the hotel with you?' I asked.

'Not sure, depends…'

'Okay, Adeboye, I'll leave you to it. I'm not having any luck so I'm going to call it a night, but speak to you soon, right?'

'Sure thang,' he said.

I left him to his beer and took a cab home. I never heard from him again.

Of course, there would also have to have been at least one British spy, maybe more, amongst the expat community in Moscow, probably even within the group I socialised with. No doubt they imagined that if no one had said anything to the contrary, they must be doing a really great job in concealing their true identity. So here's my theory: the only reason they don't get outed is because people are too scared to out them. But they're easy to spot, if you rationalise it. Think of someone in your place of work who has loads of contacts and is doing a job which actively encourages the cultivation of new friendships and connections. Maybe they're in marketing, or event management, for example. Someone who is friendly, outgoing and good with people – after all, you need to gain trust easily, right? Well, you can spot a company snitch by following your gut instinct and by keeping each piece of the jigsaw in an imaginary box at the back of your mind. So, he or she asks you a question which is not entirely relevant to the main thrust of your conversation and then asks you the same question a couple of days later, and then maybe again the following week (a three-point fact-checking exercise). He or she comes out with tiny bits of knowledge about the company that seem to be slightly less than gossip and more like informed fact (and always turn out to be true). He or she is just that little bit too eager to assert that they are 'on your side' in whatever problems you may be encountering at work. Just small things, none of which taken individually would add up to anything. But once you have saved enough jigsaw pieces in your box, you can start putting them together to come up with the full picture, and bingo! It will suddenly seem obvious who it is that's running to the boss with information on everyone else. Remember, spies are human too. Often, they will be a little frayed at the edges and may inadvertently end up letting a little steam emerge from the pressure cooker, because the concentration required to keep their double lives a secret is an emotional strain, which can get to even the most resilient of individuals.

So, spotting a company informer is surprisingly easy, and I reckon the above principles would be the same when it came to international spy rings. What isn't so easy in the latter sphere, is working out which 'side' they are on, and that's because half the time *they don't know themselves*. When your job is to immerse yourself into friendly relationships in order to garner information, eventually you begin to see the good side of the people you are associating with, and suddenly your cold and distant hardly-ever-seen spy handler from on high just doesn't seem to be as likeable any more, and the thought of betraying your new-found friends, who were not as evil as you first imagined, seems cruel and unfair. Your practical everyday experience seems more real and important than some high-flown notion of nationality and the good of the nation. And what nation is that now, anyway? Where you used to live? Or where you live now? Who's good and who's bad? Who the hell knows any more? The smaller picture becomes more relevant to you than the vague shadowy bigger picture. It's just human nature.

Imagine. A load of Western journalists are hired to work for the Kremlin's new flagship English language news channel Russia Today TV – my workplace. Are they going to instruct someone to keep an eye on the rest of us? Or course they are! And who better than a fellow foreigner, someone who walks amongst us and is accepted by us without question. Did we all suspect who he or she was within RT? Of course we did! And if that person is reading this, you'll see us all in a different light now, won't you? No one will ever say anything, but you'll see in our eyes that we've always known who you are, and nothing will ever be the same for you again. You see, there's something about treachery that stabs at the very heart of every human being. It's not your politics, it's not your views, it's not even your bosses that we so despise. It's the simple breach of trust. And, of course, the fact that you are a lying, traitorous, deceiving, two-faced scumbag (Goodness, where has all this indignant patriotism come from?). Of course, this would have to work both ways. If a bunch of Russians went to work for the BBC in London, you can guarantee that MI6 would have people tailing them too. It stands to reason, right? You might think that if I was so certain of this, I would have contacted MI6 and told them my suspicions. But what for? Here's how the conversation would go.

'Brrring, brrring. Brrring, brrring.'

(Connects).

'Hello, you have reached the offices of MI6. Press one for new recruits, press two for existing spies or press three to report a dirty snitch.'

(I press three).

'Thank you. Please wait. You will soon be put through to an operator. For training purposes this call will absolutely, no question about it, be recorded.'

(National anthem plays, until a human answers).

'Good afternoon, MI6, can I help you?'

'Yes, I'd like to report a dirty snitch who works for Russia Today TV.'

(Laughter from the other end).

'Tell us something we don't know sir.'

(Phone disconnects).

Because that's the point, isn't it? Both sides already know the identities of each other's spies, and both sides tolerate them, as long as they don't cross any unwritten lines by leaking to the media any properly important stuff. Such and such a person in the Kremlin has a penchant for sadomasochism? Yeah, that's okay. One of Russia's international envoys is an out-and-out racist? Yeah, well that's common knowledge. The exact number of nuclear warheads Russia has stationed on its territory and around the world is… 'Er, that's classified information. You have twenty-four hours to pack your bags and leave the country.' Know your enemy. I remember coming home one night to discover that the key to my apartment wouldn't work. I had put the key into the lock, but it just wouldn't turn. Odd, because the locks were a new addition to the tough security door which the landlord had proudly installed and been keen to show me. Nonetheless, I had to call him to explain the problem. He arrived and was as perplexed as I was, and not too happy at having to essentially break into his own apartment, which would soon result in even more expense in door repairs. In any case, he said he would return the next day, but for now left me inside, with just an internal bolt for security. I stood silently and looked around the apartment. Something was different. Something had changed. Something… no some*one* had been there. I could just feel it. A smell, a feeling, a whiff of violation of some kind. Slowly, I walked around, but could not find anything tangible to prove my suspicion. I just knew that someone had been there, had a good look around, and then left – unintentionally disabling the door lock in the process. Was I the enemy then? I hoped not. Was I a friend? In their eyes, maybe, but always to be watched, just in case… Anyway, back to my night out…

Following my encounter with Adeboye, I had taken a cab home, and just as I was putting my key in my front door and just when I thought the evening had finally ended, I got a text message from… Girl 5 Irina. My door was now open, key in my right hand, mobile in my left. It was 1am. The text was in broken English.

Text received: In bar. You come see? Club B2. Come to jazz.

At this hour? My mood, which had been so expensively trampled on earlier in the evening at the restaurant, had just lightened. My apartment and my exhausted body were saying, 'Go to bed.' But the excitement of Moscow was still pumping through my veins.

Text sent: Okay, I'm coming!

I entered my apartment, freshened up, and then came right back out again.

Club B2 turned out to be more than just a nightclub. It was a huge, multi-floored, multi-roomed music and dance emporium in the heart of Moscow. Like a surreal Terry Gilliam flick – imaginative, fascinating and often brilliant, though not necessarily making any sense. First, you paid an entrance fee at a security window, before passing through an airport-style metal detector. Then you had to walk through a partly open-air corridor for fifty metres or so, before arriving at another entrance. It was as if they had bought two different buildings, but couldn't quite work out how to connect them. Then, at the next entrance there was a men's cloakroom to the right and a women's one to the left. Just around the corner from the cloakrooms was a packed disco. Not a nightclub, but a disco, complete with cheesy '80s music, flashing multi-coloured lights at the DJ station and a glitter ball high above. Just next to it, a huge staircase leading up to another floor and a different music venue. This one had a band playing South American music of some description, complete with a Russian crooner and couples on the dance floor doing various versions of salsa. Then upstairs again, a larger room full of sweating teenagers doing what teenagers do – flailing around to booming nondescript massively loud and repetitive tracks, each one basically identical to the last (I was beginning to sound more and more like my parents – 'Kids these days, it's not like real music any more'). I was definitely liking this B2 place. It was akin to a journey through nightclub history down the ages, with something for everyone. And then I remembered I was supposed to be meeting Irina. But in a place this big with so many people, how was I supposed to find her? Phone her of course. I fished out my mobile. No battery. Damn. That was the thing with smartphones. If you didn't have a good one, then no girl in Moscow would take you seriously. Though smartphones do have a habit of running out of juice at the most inconvenient of moments, no matter what the blurb on the ad says.

Irina had though said something about jazz. I looked around and saw in the corner a few framed black and white photos hanging in a row on a wall, which led around the corner. On closer inspection they turned out to be prints of jazz greats. Duke Ellington, Dizzy Gillespie, Count Basie, King Curtis… they were all here, lining a red-painted corridor which presumably led to a jazz room. I followed the red brick road and sure enough it opened out into a classic jazz haunt. Sleazy, bohemian and a bit pretentious. However, it was certainly more mellow than the other sections of this musical wonderland, so I squeezed into a chair near one of the many round wooden tables and surveyed the scene. Was Irina in here somewhere? I hoped so. The band were about to start up on the small stage that the tables were arranged around and I hoped they wouldn't be too loud; it's always difficult to impress a girl when she can't hear what you're saying. Actually, it's usually difficult for me to impress them even when they *can*. And if their English isn't the best, then communication basically becomes impossible.

Still no Irina. I looked around. Groups of 20-something and 30-something Russians all out having a good time. More musically astute than you'd give them credit for. Our media would have you believe they only listen to Cossack music or something. But here they all were in tune with whatever this jazz band were about to play – a pianist, a double bass and a drummer. I glanced down at my watch. 2am now. Irina could be anywhere in this whole damn building. I looked up from my watch… and there she was! I need not have worried about her not hearing what I was saying, because we would not be talking, at least not for an hour or so. She was the singer.

I am not an expert in jazz music. I do own a saxophone and I can play a bit, but it mostly sits in the corner of the room on its stand, designed to wow girls as soon as they spot it.

'You play the saxophone!'

'Well, just a little bit, but I'm not very good,' I say, as I pick it up and play that single riff from Gerry Rafferty's 'Baker Street', which I have practised six hundred thousand times. Don't ask me to play anything else though. So like I say, it's not my forte. I know what I like and I know what I don't like. The sort of jazz that I don't understand is where they just seem to be showing off how good they are to each other, ignoring the fact that it really does help the listener if it actually sounds like music. Masturbating jazz I call it; where the audience all sit up and tap their toes like they have a clue what's going on, all pretending to be connoisseurs of the genre, nodding their heads at an impenetrable ten-minute solo section and whispering knowingly to their mates, 'Oh, he's good.'

This, however, was not that. This was a fun band who were playing timeless melodic tunes and some of their own compositions, none of which required a degree in jazz history to comprehend. Irina was a smouldering sexpot, although in the darkened hazy room I doubted that she'd spotted me. The audience were appreciative and I continued to swig from a bottle of Mexican beer which I'd ordered from the bar (how much had I drunk so far this evening?). I pondered where the tradition of putting a piece of lemon or lime in the top of the bottle actually came from. Most people think it's because of taste, but I had heard a different theory. Apparently, flies are repelled by citrus rind. Have you ever rubbed your fingers against some lemon rind and discovered how it makes the tips of your fingers feel a bit 'powdery'? Well, that's the substance that flies stay away from, because if they come into contact with it, it prevents their feet (are they called 'feet'?) from being able to stick on walls, and they hate that. Hence, they stay away from your beer. I must be drunk. And I had only just noticed that the music had stopped.

'Hi Cary!'

I looked up from my insect musings to see Irina, as sexy as you like, standing in front of me, her face flushed from the performance.

'Hi!' I said. 'Have a seat.'

She sat and regarded me.

'Great performance,' I ventured.

'Thank you. It is the jazz you like very much?' she asked in her broken English.

'Yes, but you make it sound even better.' (Pass the sick bucket). She giggled though.

'You like speed?'

Was she offering me drugs?

'Sorry?'

'The speed, you like?'

'What do you mean?'

She frowned and regarded me again.

'Um… how you say…'

'Oh, you mean the speed dating?'

'Yes!'

'Ah, yes, it was great!'

Small talk is delicate enough at the best of times, but throw in a language barrier and the opportunities for misunderstandings become far greater. My complete inability to speak Russian meant that my chances of finding a nice Russian girl whom I liked were limited by her ability to speak English. 'But that's unfair,' I hear you cry, 'You should bloody well learn to speak Russian, seeing as you are living there.' Well, yes and no. Here are the excuses as to why foreign expats living in Russia don't learn Russian.

1. It's amazingly difficult.
2. Even Russians tell you it's amazingly difficult.
3. Most expats have one-year work contracts, after which time most go back to their home countries where the usefulness of Russian is questionable, compared to French, German or Spanish, for example. With Spanish, say, you could travel around Spain (obviously), South America and much of the United States too. But Russian? Realistically, what are you going to do with that?

4. As soon as you open your mouth, Russians who have learned some English want to practise talking in English, or…

5. As soon as you open your mouth, Russians genuinely have no idea what you are saying, because it's all about emphasis. Get the pronunciation just a tiny bit wrong and you could be saying something completely different, so even trying to practise becomes frustrating. For example, a couple of days earlier, I had flagged down a cab. The driver opened the door and we started to negotiate a price for the journey. The word for '100' sounds like *'Sto'* and the word for 'What?' sounds like *'Shto?'* To me, they sound basically the same (try it yourself) but if you miss out the 'Sh' sound by mistake, this is what happens…

Driver:	*'Skolka?'* (How much?)
Me:	*'Shto.'* (thinking I had said 100, when actually I had said 'What?')
Driver:	*'Skolka?'*
Me:	*'Shto.'*
Driver:	*'Skolka?'*
Me:	*'Shto.'*
Driver:	*'Skolka?'*
Me:	*'Shto!'*
Driver:	*'Ti durak, paka!'* (You are a fool, goodbye!)

This would happen every time I tried to get a cab, until I finally twigged what was going on. Yes, it would also probably happen in China if I tried to speak Mandarin, so Russia is not alone in this. I am just offering up my excuses. Nonetheless, as I looked at the gorgeous Irina and realised she was slipping from my grasp due to a mutual lack of linguistic understanding, I decided that I would definitely start learning a few useful phrases. For cultural reasons you understand, not just to sleep with women. We agreed to meet up sometime in the future, but I got the feeling I wouldn't be seeing her again.

She went back to the stage for the second half of her set and I wondered where else this Moscow escapade was going to take me. I had been here for several months now and still my understanding of the society and its people seemed as elusive as ever. I did, however, understand that in Russia you don't always get what you see and you don't always see what you're going to get either. It was time to go home. One more wistful glance over my shoulder at Irina on stage, before making my way back, pondering over when or where I was going to meet some beautiful Russian girl whom I was going to get married to and live happily ever after with. But then maybe that was the problem. I might be in Moscow, but who said the girl of my dreams had to be Russian?

5

MULLETS AND THE BOLSHOI

'It's just men in tights, anyway!'

Foreign women usually hated Moscow. I didn't blame them really. For them, a macho culture where females appeared to them to be reduced to arm candy did not sit well with what they were accustomed to in their home countries, where they have more career opportunities and economic independence. Plus of course, British and American females, for example, who have been posted to Moscow to work for some business or other, are just as interested in some male company as males are in female company. I had no clue what the gay experience was in Moscow though – I'd heard that same-sex behaviour in the streets would not exactly be welcomed with open arms, and gay pride gatherings were usually suppressed without much restraint on behalf of the authorities, if allowed at all. Anyway, one day I overheard a British girl talking to one of her female friends in a bar.

'The trouble is, half of these Russian men have mullets and don't know how to dress,' she lamented. Her friend elaborated:

'I know, and then you've got all these amazing-looking Russian girls around, it's a disaster...'

That's not to say, of course, that British girls are ugly, it's just that when British women themselves are talking about the strength of the competition, you know they have a challenge on their hands. In the UK they have to fight off the attentions of British men, but in Moscow they are hardly noticed. The 'mullet' by the way, for those of you who are not 1970s and '80s devotees, was a hairstyle made popular in that era, mainly by British pop stars and footballers. Short at the front and sides, but very long at the back, often permed or dyed. I am not a fashion guru, but it's a style that did (and still does) look ridiculous. For reasons that I could only guess at, it was a look favoured by nearly every Russian male in Moscow. And Western females didn't like it. I did meet one woman though who was a staunch fan of Russian males – with some caveats. She was an American called Deidre. Now Deidre had been posted to Moscow as a high-flying and well-paid legal executive, but she also had a penchant for the nightlife which she blogged about on her website in the form of a fictional character, in what some would say was a rather steamy fashion – a bit too steamy for her bosses it turned out as the resulting publicity led to her being relieved of her job. Unfairly, according to her, as she felt she had been discriminated against and that her blog had had nothing to do with it, alleging that she had in fact been sexually harassed. Either way, this all led to a long drawn-out legal battle which I am definitely not going to talk about, though everything I have said so far is already in the public domain (can you tell how I am tiptoeing around it?). Anyway, given that she was still in Moscow at the time, she defiantly decided to continue writing about her tales through a local newspaper column. So instead of hiding away in shame, she put two fingers up to her former bosses and did the complete opposite by starting to live off the publicity. In fairness too, she needed the money. Now *her* opinion of Russian men seemed very different to those of her female compatriots. I met her for the first time one evening in a downtown basement bar/nightclub, where a group of foreign journalists had gathered for a few drinks and a bit of networking. The clientele included broadsheet correspondents, a couple of people from the BBC, an Irish newspaper reporter and so forth. They were all a bit dull for my liking, all going on and on about work. Journalists do have a habit of talking non-stop about their jobs, which for me is extremely boring. I wondered if accountants did the same thing. 'Oh, those figures today were at least fifty thousand out, don't you think?' Or tree surgeons. 'Wow, you should have seen the mighty oak that I had to assess today, lovely branches.' Either way, talking about one's working day usually bores me stiff, and five minutes after my arrival the first earnest journalist began to put me to sleep.

'What do you think of the president's possible choice of mayor? Will it ease the wider political situation here...?'

Zzzzzzz.

I left him with another boring journalist and went to the bar where I ordered a bottled beer and took a swig. And then I saw her. A slim-framed not very tall individual, with mousy hair and nondescript clothes, just a plain white blouse and a pair of clingy jeans. Not beautiful in the supermodel sense, yet exuding a certain other soulful beauty which made her overwhelmingly attractive, without having to dress in an overtly sexual way. And then I spotted the thing which marked her out from everyone else – she was not wearing any shoes. Completely barefoot in a nightclub. Maybe she was having a rest from aching stilettos, or maybe she just liked it. Well I liked it too; it just added to the intrigue. I sidled over, deciding to ignore her lack of shoes as a conversation starter, given that every other bloke had probably already quizzed her on that. Our conversation went something like this:

'Hi, I'm Cary.'

'Deidre,' she replied, hand extended, in an accent which revealed her New York roots.

'So, what are you doing these days here in Moscow?' I asked.

'Oh, some writing, you know.'

I decided to steer away from the obvious question, by *not* asking her what sort of writing she did.

'What do you think of Russian guys?' I asked.

Her eyes lit up, as it was clearly a subject she was familiar with, and enthusiastic about.

'I kinda like them. They have a manliness about them that you don't get with Western guys. There's no messing about, you know? If they feel like physically whisking you off your feet and carrying you across a puddle, they'll just do it!' she laughed.

'Don't Western guys do that too?' I asked.

'Hell, no! Most of them, you know, would get a hernia or something. And I have to say, when it comes to taking all day to make a move on a girl, you Brits are the worst. It's like (she put on a mock British accent), "Oh, sorry, could I possibly, er, well, you know, perhaps you wouldn't mind if I, kind of maybe removed your brassiere, er..." It's so funny.'

She laughed again, and I agreed with her in that typically British self-deprecating kind of way.

'So are you saying that Ruskie guys are a bit rough and ready?'

'Well, if you want to put it like that. But you kinda know what you're getting and they buy you roses and stuff, 'cos they know how to court women and make grand gestures. It's like men are men, and women are women. Though they can be abusive, so you have to be careful.'

She flicked a look to the bar.

'The thing is, I can't really talk to you right now,' she whispered conspiratorially.

'Why not?'

'Because my Russian companion won't really like it. They get very jealous you know.'

Now she tells me. I looked up, and sure enough her burly Russian hunk of a companion was indeed just returning from the bar with drinks, looking somewhat displeased that his American trophy girl was apparently cavorting with a foreigner. I leaned closer.

'If it doesn't work out, I'd love to take you out on a date,' I whispered, half-jokingly.

'Ha ha, maybe another time,' she countered, completely unfazed by my clumsy advance. And then she was gone. An eloquent and intelligent lady, contemplating life and love in a fascinating, yet sometimes scary environment. It was time to make myself scarce. I had at least discovered the view of Russian men from a different perspective and it had been a refreshing vignette. And did I fancy her? God yes, but it wasn't to be.

Soon after, I met another woman, whom I shall call Emma, who also happened to be from the States. Emma was an athletic, good-looking, thirty-something woman, with honey-blonde hair, brown eyes and a pleasant manner about her, albeit with the usual slightly too loud American voice (American cousins, why must you *shout* all the time?). She also had two little dachshunds, one of which was blind poor thing, though dogs rely much more heavily on their sense of smell than their sight. Emma and I had met in a bar by the banks of the Moscow River and I had asked her out to dinner. After two dates, she had invited me back to hers for an 'American evening', she'd said. Just me and her plus her two little pooches, popcorn, hot dogs, nachos with cheese sauce all over them, and a night in watching an American football game on cable TV, which had been specially installed for her. Now, to my mind, American football is the most boring game on earth. All those guys with all that padding and helmets. Why do they need them? No one wears padding in rugby and let me tell you, those rugby blokes are monsters. And have you ever seen Aussie rules football? To the uninitiated, there appear to be hardly any rules at all – just huge guys slugging it out. Can you imagine one of them saying, 'Oh, I just need to wear a pad because the last time you hit me, it hurt a bit.' Plus, the American game stops and starts the whole time, even pausing at some points to allow adverts to be broadcast on the telly, so that viewers at home don't miss any of the so-called action. Ridiculous. Nonetheless, here we were, two Westerners enjoying the 'special relationship' of having a similar language and more or less similar tastes. As we sat there on her sofa, she tried her best to explain what was going on, while her doggies snuggled up between us. Actually, I just wanted the doggies to bugger off so that I could get my paws on Emma. But no, they stayed, and Emma and I were reduced to just chatting. Not exactly 'Touchdown!' but that's just how it was. Sadly, we never met again. A misunderstanding over who was supposed to text whom over meeting up next, and somehow it didn't happen. It was just one of those brief and strange liaisons that can occur when two fish out of water find themselves, well, out of water. And that was that. My quest for a soulmate would have to continue.

On a scale of one to ten, as far as being in touch with their feminine side goes, Russian men come in at zero. For them, anything that smacks of being non-macho is wayward at best and downright unnatural at worst, and thus far I had not been contradicted by what I had seen, or by what Deidre and others had told me. Russian men were, however, extremely practical. I had not come across a Russian man who didn't know how to put up shelves, or change a tyre, or handle a drill. With a historical lack of opportunities in terms of job prospects and promotion, practical skills had to be learned from necessity, so you could at least earn some money from being able to turn your hand to virtually anything. And goodness me, do they love drills. Every man had a drill and every man was using it to renovate an apartment and annoy everyone else living within a mile radius, for months on end. It's as if they didn't realise that to paint a wall, all you needed was paint and a paintbrush; somehow they would always find a way of incorporating the use of a drill, like some kind of twenty-first century Excalibur. Still, what does a girl prefer, a practical man who can put stuff up, or a guy like me who wouldn't know a drill bit from a chisel?

Anyway, they were all happy to embroil themselves in endless DIY projects, like kids with new toys at Christmas. It was partly because many of the people who owned apartments in Moscow actually got properties given to them for free on the break-up of the Soviet Union. Places that used to belong to the state suddenly belonged to the officials who were previously only just caretakers. Then they just started passing them on to their sons and daughters. So there was a whole tranche of Russians who owned properties without actually understanding the concept of property ownership, in terms of working for it, saving up for it and finally buying it. For the elite, having an apartment or two was just like being given a set of crystal glasses that have always been in the family. Nice, but what exactly do you do with them? Just keep them for show, or put them to some kind of use?

Bang! Bang! Bang! Rrrrrrrrrrrrr!

The nightmare of hammering and drilling was back, this time next to my new apartment. But it wasn't just one apartment. Someone or some company had decided to erect a whole *block* of apartments, right next door. They were building in a gaping chasm between my block of apartments and the adjacent block. I had often noticed a few mechanical diggers and workers wandering around there and thought that maybe they were going to put some tarmac down for a car park perhaps. In fact, I was told there used to be a block of apartments there, but one day the owners decided to renovate the basement area, in order to create some parking space. Unfortunately, they didn't support the walls properly while the work was taking place, and the whole building collapsed. Some poor Caucasus workers had been crushed to death in the incident. It was also the case that across the city, Moscow was struggling with the weight of its own buildings. Apart from the Metro, there was also a vast underground network of secret tunnels built by Stalin, designed to make sure that the dictator and his minions would still survive in the event of a nuclear attack. And I mean a *vast* set of tunnels. Some of it was even open for tourists to view, but most of it remained much as it did all those years ago – dark, dank and smelly. Of course, it meant that when they tried to dig foundations for new buildings, often they just sank into an unexpected tunnel. There was also considerable erosion caused by underground rivers which was making the situation far worse. The result was the odd building spontaneously falling down, like some kind of contagious concrete suicide. So when the noisy, heavy-duty diggers arrived and the fumes from the electric generators started to fill my apartment night and day, I knew it was time to move on again, though I soon found a new place. A modern, convenient apartment, just ten minutes' walk to work and reasonably priced too. But that didn't last long either, due to a peculiar quirk of Russian culture – they don't negotiate. I'd only been in the pad for a month when the landlady decided to pay me a visit.

'I am making a small adjustment to the rent. We agreed 50,000 roubles a month. It is now 60,000 roubles.'

The equivalent of one hundred pounds was hardly a 'small adjustment'. And that was it. No negotiation or chitchat. Not:

'Hi Cary, we need to discuss the rent and come to some sort of agreement due to a sudden change of circumstances.'

'Okay landlady, well maybe if the rent goes up, you could install a new cooker for me because this one is a bit old?'

'Well, let's see what we can do and come to a compromise...'

No, nothing like that. I point-blank refused of course. Hilariously, she looked surprised when I told her I was leaving, having just moved in.

'Cary, why you leave?'

'Because you've put the rent up after a month.'

'Yes, but why you leave?' she asked again, seemingly genuinely puzzled.

The Russian rouble had (as it does periodically) taken a turn for the worse, and Russians have no faith in their own currency. She saw it as natural that the rent would shoot up. But it was also about saving face. Russians do not, above anything else, want to appear weak – from an apartment landlord, right up to the president. Weakness is not an option, and haggling is seen as a sign of weakness. Imagine what those political summit meetings must be like with the Americans, themselves not the greatest diplomats in the world. What fun that must be:

(American) 'If you want to keep your influence over Ukraine, we're going to put some missiles in Poland.'

(Russian) '*Nyet.*'

(American) 'Well, how about we reduce some military bases, but we get to keep the oil in Afghanistan?'

(Russian) '*Nyet.*'

(American) 'Okay, well maybe instead we keep our fingers in South America and you get Africa.'

(Russian) '*Nyet.*'

(American) 'Well, how about we kick your ass from here to Albuquerque, you communist assholes!'

(Russian) '*Nyet.*'

And so it was time to pack my bags yet again and find another apartment – hopefully less noisy and less expensive.

My new place was right next to the Canadian Embassy in the centre of town. I always feel a bit sorry for Canadians. No one really knows what they're about or takes them very seriously. When you think of America you think of the Statue of Liberty, Miami Beach, yellow New York taxis, American football (loved by millions, despite leaving me nonplussed), Coca-Cola, great hospitality and *in-yer-face* friendly people. Cultural icons and traits, which whether you love them or hate them, still defined the country's image at home and abroad. At least they have an identity. But when you think of Canada, you think of... what? Mounties in red uniforms, and that's about it. Oh, and part of the population speaks French. That's not to say that visitors don't like it there. How does the saying go? 'Canada is like America, but without all the Americans.' I mean, I too had visited Canada (admittedly only Toronto) and found it to be clean, modern and friendly, but frankly a bit dull. Anyway, back to its embassy in Moscow, with its big red and white Canadian maple leaf flag unfurled out the front and its 24-hour security booths by the entrance, with hired Russian security guys who would eyeball you with suspicion every time you walked by. They would come out and check under every parked car, anywhere remotely near the embassy, with those telescopic under-car mirrors. I always wondered why anyone would have a gripe against the Canadians, as they never really seemed to get involved in much, unlike their more gung-ho southern cousins.

Anyway, I was moving into a small but perfectly formed seventh-floor apartment within a block that had a minuscule lift in the centre, like one of those old black-and-white film lifts I mentioned earlier, with a see-through cage. I kept expecting to see Audrey Hepburn or Cary Grant coming out of the lift (the latter was whom I was named after – my mum being a fan of old Hollywood flicks). Having moved all my belongings in and handed over my roubles to my new landlady (a 30-something businesswoman, who had been awarded the apartment as part of a divorce settlement), I decided to go food shopping. On my return I had five bulging bags of potatoes, rice, cabbages and vodka, which I set down next to the old cranky lift shaft. I punched the button and watched while the steel levers and cogs creaked slowly into action, as the lift shuddered its way down the hardly big enough square chute, before landing with a 'clunk' next to me on the ground floor. I shoved the steel cage apart, then the internal wooden door, before squeezing all my shopping and myself into the tiny space within. I bet Cary Grant never had to do this. The lift stopped at the seventh floor, but then nothing happened. The internal door was supposed to open automatically. I looked at the bank of grimy buttons and lights on the panel. They'd all gone dead, and no amount of levering the door on my part made any difference. I was stuck. In some panic, I stabbed at the alarm button, but nothing happened. I then started shouting for help, but it was the middle of the day, so no one was around. Great. Locked inside a lift in Moscow. Peering through the bars, I could see all the way down to the ground floor, experiencing that odd dizzying perspective you get when you look over the edge of a precipice. I was gripped by the sudden fear that whatever was holding the lift up would suddenly snap and I would plummet, screaming all the way to my certain death at the bottom. So what to do? I crouched down around the shopping bags, knees up and back against the wall. Time passed and still no one had turned up in any of the other apartments. I was now hungry and thirsty. I opened up a shopping bag and began chewing on a piece of cabbage. I wondered how long it would be before I could stomach a raw potato. I looked at the bottles of vodka. Well, why not? I was in Moscow after all. I started swigging. Vodka and cabbage. It was probably what most of the countryside population survived on during the Second World War, so who was I to complain? Trouble is, it was making me even thirstier and at some point, I would have to urinate. Oh God, what if I needed to poo? Two hours and still no one, and now I was also drunk. I waited for what seemed like an age, before suddenly I heard footsteps coming up the stairs! I looked out through the steel cage to see an old lady making her way up slowly. Saved! I shouted to her as she approached my level, but when she finally got to my floor, huffing and puffing, she started scolding me. It was something on the lines of:

'You drunk idiot, you have broken the lift!'

She carried on up the stairs, went into her apartment and closed the door, leaving me to my fate.

'You stupid old hag!' I shouted.

I then started laughing, probably more in nervous fear than any real mirth. I just could not believe what she had done. A few minutes later, though, I really was saved. A lone guy coming home from work spotted me with my vodka and cabbages and immediately winched open the doors from the outside. He was completely matter-of-fact about it. Not one word. No drama. As if this was a daily occurrence (maybe it was). I spilled out of the lift and onto the landing, along with rolling cabbages and the clink of vodka bottles on the concrete. He silently went on his way, while I contemplated the joys of freedom.

It was never clear who you were supposed to call when communal things broke down. Back in Soviet days it was all done by the state, but with Russia's recently discovered quasi-democratic credentials, no one knew who was officially supposed to do what, and who got paid for what and by whom. So if the lift broke down, some dusty old workman would arrive a few days later to cobble some bits of cable together with a few rusty old bolts and – Hey presto! – the lift would work again after a fashion, until the next time it shuddered to a halt. I gathered up my shopping and went gratefully into my apartment.

There were always Russian film crews hanging around outside my block, and given that the building looked decidedly run-down and unremarkable from the outside, I couldn't work out what it was they had actually come to see. It turned out that a fat, retired, jaundiced, alcoholic Soviet film editor lived in squalor on the ground floor with his even fatter drooling dog and a roomful of ancient film equipment. Every now and then a film crew would turn up to interview him about the old days of the Soviet film industry, while his jowly dog licked its own balls in the corner. He once allowed me to watch one of these interviews being filmed. The crew were reverential and in complete awe, as if he were some kind of celluloid godfather. He talked to them with authority and candour while swigging vodka, his bulbous nose needing to be powdered by the make-up team on a regular basis, between coughing fits brought on by the endless cigarettes he smoked and stubbed out in a cracked and ash-laden saucer. He talked about Soviet-era productions like *Ivan the Terrible,* and *Cossacks of the Kuban,* describing how the film-makers often had to hide the true meaning of their work through subplots and disguised themes, in order to avoid the heavy hand of the censor. I could only translate fragments of what he was saying in his very slow Russian delivery.

'It is happening again,' he wheezed between fags. 'The censors are creeping back like frost over the great Russian landscape.' Or something like that.

He related how in later years the industry won great praise with productions like *Come and See,* a film about Nazi atrocities in villages of the then Byelorussian Soviet Socialist Republic, and the 1972 psychological science-fiction drama *Solaris,* which to this day remains the most boring film I have ever tried to watch – I've tried twice and still can't get to the end without falling asleep.

As I watched the interview, I wondered how much he got paid for his trouble. I suspected he would have been just as happy with the occasional case of vodka and a crate of cigarettes to help him through his days of wallowing around the dimly lit corridors and stairs of the building that I now called home. Moscow buildings were certainly varied to say the least. Old wooden constructions with tin roofs and great charm, sitting uncomfortably side by side with hideous grey concrete monoliths, or maybe glittering historic Orthodox Church domes adjacent to ultra-modern apartments. For too many years, buildings were constructed for short-term financial gain, rather than any long-term consideration for the design and heritage of the city. In its haste to become modern and dynamic, Moscow ran before it could walk, leading to the inevitable planning and construction absurdities. Some buildings were deliberately left to disintegrate on their own, so that corrupt town hall officials could then designate them as being 'unsafe' and were able to then knock them down (for a fat backhander) to be replaced by more lucrative blocks of apartments or business premises. Often the existing residents were told to get out or face being swept away with the bricks and mortar when the bulldozers arrived. In fairness, some people were offered alternative accommodation, but usually a good distance outside the city. A case of 'take it or leave it'. There were campaign groups who had tried to prevent all this from happening, but with limited success. More recently, however, the new Mayor of Moscow seemed to be signalling a reversal of this policy. Too late for those buildings that had already been flattened, but not too late perhaps for those that remained. Though as soon as he'd got his feet under the table, he awarded a street paving contract, worth millions of roubles, to a company which just happened to be owned by... his wife. What a coincidence.

There was a small, ornate, derelict building on my street, which was a classic example of architectural oddness. Its doors and windows seemingly constructed during a time when people were smaller and shorter. There were crumbling carved symbols above the entrance, apparently of a Masonic nature. Yet at night there always remained one stray light bulb eerily illuminating the inside of one of the ground-floor rooms. Perhaps the previous Masonic occupants had forgotten to turn it off in their haste to finish rolling up their trouser legs, giving each other funny handshakes and sacrificing chickens, or whatever it is that Masons do. It was a nice old building though, and a real shame to see it in such a state. One building, however, that had certainly been restored to its former glory was the Bolshoi Theatre, the headquarters if you can call it that of the world-famous Bolshoi Ballet. The restoration project had overrun its budget by *billions* of roubles, but then I don't remember that daft Millennium Dome in London being cheap, and what major project ever comes in under budget anyway? At least the Russians had made a good fist of it and it really did look great – huge imposing pillars on the outside, with grand and magnificent designs on the inside. The ballet holds a special place in Russians' hearts, probably because it always seems to be about angst, tragedy, regret, and the striving for something that is often unattainable. It seemed to strike a chord with them, from dancers like Irina Baronova in the 1930s, to Rudolf Nureyev (who later defected to the West) to more recent stars like Diana Vishneva and Daniil Simkin. A symbol of expression during a time when expression was repressed, the ballet had become an enduring part of Russian culture and pride, with more meaning to audiences here than those who attended the ballet in the West. I remember once how many years ago the Bolshoi Ballet appeared in a special touring performance of *Swan Lake* in a huge marquee in London's Hyde Park. I had been invited by a friend and her father who had bought the tickets. When we got there, it was a magnificent sight. It was less of a marquee and more of a wonderful fairy tale canvas structure held up by strategically placed struts and poles. Before the show began, the lighting was already atmospheric – blue spotlights shining through synthetic smoke as the buzz of expectation spread among the well-dressed and excited crowd. My friend's dad had been waxing lyrical for weeks.

'The ballet is fantastic you know, especially the Bolshoi; the Russians are such wonderfully artistic technicians…'

There was certainly a degree of snobbery about the event. Anyone who had been lucky enough to get one of the outlandishly expensive tickets was suddenly an expert on ballet.

'I just love their light-footedness, the Russian girls are delightful and the male dancers are just exceptional…' he went on.

Picking our way past those who were already seated, we found our places, halfway back from the stage, and began to settle in. But then, a howl of indignation from my friend's father.

'I'm right behind a pole! I can't see anything!' he exclaimed.

It was true. His view was severely restricted by one of the struts holding up the marquee. The lights went down and the crowd went silent as the much-publicised Russian extravaganza was about to begin. Except that the silence and darkness was abruptly shattered by one angry voice. My friend's father, still infuriated by his seat placement, stood up and addressed the entire auditorium.

'It's just men in tights anyway!' he bellowed at the top of his voice.

All his previously little-known appreciation of the great Bolshoi Ballet, forgotten in an instant. There was shock and outrage from the assembled crowd, as he continued his tirade.

'Ballet is just for ponces!'

'Dad, for God's sake, sit down!' my friend hissed in vain. But it was no good – he continued his rant until security arrived to escort him away, as the curtain rose for the performance to begin. The men-in-tights crusader had been silenced, and while the show itself turned out to be fantastic, I couldn't help thinking that the pre-show drama had been even more entertaining. Let's be honest, ballet does go on a bit, and I always wondered if the Russian performers waiting in the wings were using their time thinking more about how they could abscond from the troupe and stay in the West, and less about their next part on stage.

Anyway, here in Russia, it wasn't so much about the snobbery of the event, but more about the ballet itself. I knew nothing about the technical stuff, but all the spinning around, tip-toeing and hoisting into the air looked pretty good to me and the audience were taking it deadly seriously, some even shedding tears at the end. The heyday of the Bolshoi Ballet was supposed to be in the past, but from where I was sitting I'd say it was alive and kicking today. Although I'm sure a couple of the male dancers were sporting mullets, or was that part of their costume? As the cast took their bows, they were showered with sweet-smelling red roses from all sides in a genuine show of affection. And as I left the auditorium with the aroma still in my nostrils and the tide of emotions continuing to wash over me, I felt uplifted and full of life. However, a person's well-being is often only as good as their ability to experience it. Without your health you begin to question the point of it all, as I was about to discover.

6

DON'T GET SICK IN RUSSIA

'I pulled my trousers down and stood in what I imagined
to be a confident pose, like some kind of porn star'

It was the 1st of June – the month when all work contracts
for foreigners were renewed, or not as the case may be,
and although my contract was not yet up for renewal, I
still had to go through the procedures as though I was a
new employee in order to update my contract for a further
six months, because all contracts had to be synchronised
from the 1st of June, no matter what, even if you'd only
joined two weeks ago. Why? 'Don't ask, this is Russia.' Or
one theory I had heard was that if they renewed foreigners'
contracts at the end of December, during the vicious
winter, they would lose far more employees than during
the milder month of June. Either way, the procedures

involved going to a Soviet-style hospital where you would be given a medical test. All foreigners had to undergo a yearly HIV test if they wanted to stay in the country.

Anyway, I was instructed to go to a Russian hospital, which was exactly how I imagined it would be. Bare, dilapidated, stern and concrete. The hospital didn't have a name, just a number; labelled and catalogued in accordance with Soviet procedure – and of course, inexplicable in its workings. At the front desk, one of the miserable old receptionists gave me a look sourer than a wrinkled lime.

'Name?'

I told her.

'Company?'

I told her.

'Fill out form.'

She handed over a form for me to sign at the bottom, on which was written several different door numbers with a Russian blurb printed next to each one. Clearly, I was meant to go on a little tour of the hospital with the task of finding each door, behind which would be a different doctor representing a different test. So blood test, X-ray and so forth.

'Thanks,' I said, receiving not a flicker in response.

Finding each door was the first challenge. There seemed to be no particular numbering system in place and every door was on a different level. Once located, I then had to negotiate the gaggle of patients all massing around each door, clutching similar bits of paper and trying to get in. I quickly realised that if you stood around waiting 'in line' you would soon discover that there *was* no line. It was just a matter of who shouted the loudest, or who gave the impression of being the most important. I had, though, experienced something like this before, on a trip to India. I had been trying to buy a train ticket from the main station in New Delhi. Even though I had managed to elbow my way to the counter, there was still a mass of noisy people pushing and shoving all around, and I had to literally cling to the counter to remain in position.

'I'd like to buy a ticket for the first-class carriage please!' I yelled.

'No sir, you have to buy a second-class ticket,' the attendant had replied, smiling.

'But you do have first-class tickets, don't you?'

'Yes sir.'

'Well, can I buy one please?' I asked desperately, as the sea of people began to push me away, like a surfer succumbing to a perilous wave.

'No sir, you have to buy a second-class ticket.'

'Why?'

'You just have to.'

At that stage, as a foreigner abroad you have to stand back and take your medicine, and as the shoving continued around me, I thrust some rupees in his direction and bought the undesired second-class ticket. Much later, I became aware that on that particular day, on that particular train for whatever reason, the only way to obtain a first-class ticket was to buy a second-class one, get on the train, and then slip a few rupees to the attendant to get into the first-class carriage. Not quite the system I was used to, but at least it was a system of sorts. India and Russia did seem to have an unlikely connection in that sense, and indeed politically they seemed very amicable with each other, for no particular historical or cultural reasons that I could fathom – just a mutual understanding of how not to queue. Here in the Russian hospital, the principle appeared to be the same; I would have to get around the thronging mass of patients by exerting my imagined authority. Hopefully, I wouldn't have to part with any roubles.

'I'm from Russia Today TV, Russia Today TV!' I bellowed.

It seemed to do the trick. The masses reluctantly parted for me and I thrust my paper at the nearest nurse. She ushered me into a small room, scrutinised the sheet, then motioned for me to stand up.

'Down, down!' she said.

I sat down.

'No, up, up!'

I stood up.

'Down, down!' she motioned with her hand.

I sat. What was this, a test of reaction times?

She did not look amused though and went off to consult with someone. When she came back, having gleaned the correct English word from a colleague, she tried again.

'Up, up,' she motioned.

I stood up.

'Now, down, down, *trousers* down!'

Oh right! I pulled my trousers down and stood in what I imagined to be a confident pose, like some kind of porn star. She had a good look at my nether regions while writing a few notes, then motioned the trousers up again. What on earth had she been looking for? Was that the test for sexually transmitted diseases, a quick glance? It appeared so. I subsequently found out that none of my work colleagues had got the trousers down treatment that day. Perhaps she just wanted to see for herself if a certain racial stereotype was true – if so, I'm not so sure she'd have been satisfied by what she'd seen. Anyway, that ticked, next stop: the drugs and alcohol doctor. This was to determine whether I was a drug addict or an alcoholic. The doctor turned out to be an affable fellow with a bushy brown moustache, wearing a shabby white lab coat, who had learnt one English adjective and was sticking to it.

'Tremendous!' he smiled.

'Er… yes, I suppose so,' I said, wondering what he was getting at.

'Whisky?'

'Sorry?'

'You drink whisky?'

'No.'

He frowned, as his hand hovered over my form.

'Vodka?'

'No.'

Another frown.

'Beer?'

'Yes, sometimes.'

'Tremendous!'

He scribbled this down on the bit of paper, stamped it, then motioned me out. It seemed he had to put *something* on the paper otherwise his job would not exist. A case of, 'I've examined him and discovered he drinks a bit, but is not an alcoholic.' That was it. Next stop, the X-ray department. The drugs and booze doctor had simply motioned me to go through a door, which led to... an outside courtyard. Wondering if I had taken the wrong door, I ventured across the yard to another building, only to be motioned by a receptionist back outside to... the same courtyard. Had I missed something? It turned out that I had. The 'X-ray department' was in fact a small ramshackle caravan in the middle of the courtyard. I knocked on the door of the caravan. It was swung open from the inside by a wiry, grey-haired old guy with a mug of coffee in one hand and a half-smoked cigarette in the other.

'Da, da,' (Yes, yes) he said, motioning me inside. The interior looked as though he had been living there all his life. Faded net curtains, a worn red flowery carpet, a small sink with a battered old kettle nearby and dirty cups everywhere. Exactly as you would imagine a caravan inhabited by a hermit, except perhaps for the worryingly old and decrepit-looking X-ray machine wedged into the corner. It had to be something from the 1950s. Unreal. I wondered how safe it was. Not very, I concluded seconds later. Still, I was in the system now, so there was no turning back. I presented my bit of paper to him and he waved me to the back, insisting I took off my shirt and thrust my chest right up against the cold vertical slab of the X-ray machine. Cancer, here I come.

Whrrrr, clunk!

The machine had done its invasive work and I don't care how safe scientists say X-ray machines are, because if the dosage of radiation is as low as they tell us, then how come doctors, nurses and dentists all leave the room before switching the machine on with a remote control? Well, anyway, my bit of paper had now been fully stamped, so I handed it back to the receptionist and made my way out and home. Little did I know I would be right back in hospital just a day later.

I had noticed a swelling between the base of my penis and my abdomen. A worryingly painful and swollen whoknowswhat? Time to see the doctors who I had already so roundly criticised, and put my trust in pills and conventional medicine. Maybe instead I should have sought the services of herbalists, acupuncturists, aromatherapists and other '-ists' who we are so ferociously instructed to regard as cranks. I remember going to the doctor in the UK once about some minor ailment or other.

'Are you taking any medication at the moment?' he'd asked me.

'Well, only some turmeric tablets for some acid indigestion, and since I've been taking them, I haven't had a problem for more than a year.'

A faint condescending smirk had come over his face.

'Is that some kind of *herbal* thing?'

'Er, yes I suppose so, but it's working.'

He smiled, whilst scribbling something on his prescription pad.

'Here, take some of these pills.'

Incredible. There I was telling him I hadn't had a problem for more than a year, yet still he dismissed my 'herbal' remedy as though I was a peasant from the Middle Ages. Anyway… I went to see a Russian surgeon who took one look at my swollen area and said, 'Hernia.' For the medically uninitiated, which I certainly was, it meant that a piece of my intestine was sticking out through a rip in my abdominal wall, and if it didn't get sorted out, it could completely rupture, leading to possible strangulation of the intestine and a nasty blue-faced death.

So, within just a couple of days, I was being wheeled on my back on a hospital bed into an operating room of what was supposed to be one of Moscow's top medical centres, a private hospital designed to attract gullible expats into thinking that its glossy interior and bustling friendly staff meant that the treatment they received there would be better than a traditionally Soviet centre. It didn't. In fact, I subsequently heard stories of expats being diagnosed with all sorts of illnesses needing radical treatment, only to take the diagnosis back to the UK and be told there was nothing wrong with them at all. Was it a case of doing things to you in order to reap the insurance money? It certainly seemed like it, but at the time, what did I know?

It's a scary thing an operation. You're made to be unconscious, and despite all the assurances, you always wonder, 'Will I wake up?' Especially as you've just been handed a form to sign which basically says, 'If anything goes wrong, the surgeon, assistants, hospital and all the shareholders bear no responsibility whatsoever for your accidental death, even if it's obviously our fault.

Additionally, we will do our best to cover up or ignore any wrongdoing or professional incompetence.'

From my back, looking upwards, it was just as I imagined it would be. Assistants with green plastic hats and mouth covers, with big surgical light bulb arrays shining down and a machine next to me that went 'blip' every other second. The only difference was that they were speaking in Russian. The anaesthetist had already pricked the vein in my arm and I was about to ask the surgeon how long it was going to take for me to...

I opened my eyes, still on my back. Groggy and disoriented, vaguely aware of hospital staff milling around the bedside, babbling in Russian. General anaesthetic seems to take about half a second to work, yet a lot longer to recover from. Damn, I never got to ask my question. Vaguely aware of something cold by my abdomen and something in my arm. Feeling tired and unable to move. Slipping away again...

This time when I woke up, I was a bit more aware of my surroundings. A standard Russian hospital bed, a drip thingy in my left arm and a hospital room that contained just one other bed, with an old guy asleep (or dead?) in it. The walls were a light shade of lime green, seemingly a default colour in Russia for the interior of any institution. There was an old TV perched on a rickety frame on the wall in front, and to my left a large window which looked out on to three grey apartment blocks. To my right, a small hospital trolley. Very slowly, I peeled back the sheet with my right hand to reveal a large ice pack over the bit where they had sliced me open down below. And goodness me, did it hurt. A stinging, burning pain that made me question if I would ever walk again. What misery.

A nurse arrived with a tray of seriously unappetising food, which she placed on the trolley. I was not allowed to have anything spicy, due to the fact that the surgery had involved shoving around a bit of my intestine, which would still be a bit delicate. So what was congealed on the plate was a kind of white meatball and a splurge of insipid mashed potato. Ugh. But I was hungry, so forced it down nonetheless. My room-mate was also awake (not dead after all). His name was Anatoly. A small, grey-haired Russian man in his nineties, who spoke very little English, wore too much aftershave and had just had a hip replacement. Despite his stature and age, there was something strong and resilient about him and I subsequently found out he was an ex-army man of some description who had seen action. He would spend the time in his hospital bed reading books about the Second World War, his gold-rimmed glasses perched on the end of his nose, before falling asleep and snoring like a foghorn. Then when he woke up and fancied a little walk, he would grab his Zimmer frame with both hands and lift it, before placing it down a few inches ahead, and then dragging his own feet forward, in a slow regular shuffle, the metallic frame making a distinctive sound as it hit the ground.

Clack! Shuffle. Pause.

Clack! Shuffle. Pause.

Given that he had just had a hip replacement, his speed of recovery was astonishing for a man of his age,

I thought. That day, the surgeons, accompanied by their assistants and students, arrived on their daily rounds to check on our respective progress. I complained bitterly about the pain and my inability to walk, while Anatoly looked on with interest from his bed. The medical staff then turned their attentions to him, saying he needed to rest and to make sure he took his medication at regular times precisely as instructed. He nodded his head sagely and said some stuff in Russian on the lines of, 'Yes doctor, you are right, I will do as you say.'

The minute the gaggle of medics left, however, he motioned to them dismissively.

'What do those idiot doctors know? They weren't even born when I joined the army.'

He motioned for me to get out of bed, and with a mischievous look in his eyes showed me a secret stash of cigarettes which he had ferreted in from somewhere and was hiding in his hospital gown. I realised that his daily shuffling walks were less about recuperation and more about sneaking out for a secret puff somewhere in the hospital grounds. He motioned to me.

'Up, up! Yes, up, up!'

Despite the pain, I was determined to do my best. I felt like a new and rather soft army recruit who didn't want to disappoint his superior and needed to toughen up fast. Over the next few days, I would shuffle along with him down the corridor, into the lift and down to the basement, where he'd discovered a seldom used service entrance. We would stand outside in front of a little area of greenery and trees. When you've been stuck inside a hospital room for several days (my hernia was taking longer to heal than expected), the sight of a few trees and the sound of birds chirping has a remarkably therapeutic effect. My army room-mate knew what he was talking about. Sure, his smoking habit was a bit of an irony given where we were, but he'd seen all of life, and death too I imagined, and was helping me to recover my sense of emotional and physical well-being and perspective.

We shuffled back to our room. By this time, I had realised that I was... ahem... unable to poo. It had been days since the surgery and still nothing. I felt bloated and horrid. I described my symptoms to the nearest nurse, and within two minutes she had returned with a long plastic tube attached to a huge bag of clear liquid.

'Turn over.'

Oh my God, I thought. I was suddenly going to be subjected to colonic irrigation, without even so much as an explanation or a reassuring, 'Don't worry, it will all be fine.' Just a stern, 'Turn over.' I had heard that this can be extremely painful, let alone the awful humiliation, but here goes...

I turned around and without further ado the nurse essentially shoved the tube up my butt right there in front of Anatoly (no thought of providing privacy) and started injecting the liquid. It felt cold and weird, but so far, no pain. I'm sure Anatoly had seen a lot worse in the field of action, so no embarrassment on his part. When she had finished, I felt nothing, and no movement from my bowels either.

'Five minutes, you go toilet.'

I decided to go to the toilet straight away, just in case, and just sat there on the loo of this Moscow hospital, waiting to expunge the contents of my colon, with the hernia pain still searing into my side. What strange situations we end up in during the course of our lives (still nothing down below). I wondered how people coped with being stuck in this kind of sterile hospital environment for long-term sicknesses. A hospital is like an enclosed mini-social environment in its own right. All sorts of weird and wonderful characters, rules to be broken, favourite areas, food and cleaning schedules, and a whole other list of social hierarchies and behaviours which... (uh-oh, here it comes). Suddenly, I had no control of my bottom department. It just wouldn't stop streaming out. How much shit can one person contain? Yet, once it was all done (after about ten minutes) it felt marvellous! Let me tell you, colonic irrigation is great. The relief of not being bloated like a Zeppelin is fantastic!

So, it was back to bed with a smile. Anatoly looked up from his bed with a knowing smirk. Despite having had major surgery, he somehow still managed to maintain neat and tidy bedsheets, with the covers precisely turned over and under at the sides, with not a crease in sight, army style. Mine was always a mess. Soon, he had dispensed with the Zimmer and was just using two crutches, which in no time he had reduced to one. What an inspiration.

'You like cigarettes, you like to smoke?' he asked.

'Well, I prefer beer really.'

He laughed and shuffled off for another puff, leaving me alone in the room to ponder my slow recovery. The surgeons here were like many other public service professionals in Russia: authoritative and uncommunicative. Hence, I had received no information before the surgery and no information after it either. Not a thing. For all I knew, the surgeon (a dismissive, patronising little man) had cut me open, watched an episode of *Russia's Got Talent*, had a few drinks, then stitched me up again. There was no patient-doctor relationship at all. Therefore, the fact that my hernia operation seemed to be taking ages to heal was all the more worrying. I couldn't help thinking that maybe I should have got it done back in Britain. People in the UK moan endlessly about the National Health Service and its perceived deficiencies. Well, after this experience I can assure them they have little to moan about.

Thud! Shuffle. Pause.

Thud! Shuffle. Pause.

This was now the new sound that Anatoly made with his one rubber-bottomed crutch to get around. He had returned to our room after his usual tobacco break and hauled himself back into bed – a waft of smoke-impregnated clothes and his usual overpowering aftershave assaulting my nostrils. Yet, I was pleased to see him back. He reached for the TV remote control, and the box on the wall flickered into life. Some Russian football was on. A repeat of some old match between Spartak Moscow and Zenit Saint Petersburg, with an excitable Russian commentator describing the details of the game, with the occasional English word thrown in like, 'Penalty!' Some words seem to be universal, especially when it comes to football. As we watched in silence, Anatoly slowly reached into the pocket of his hospital gown and like a magician revealing a dove, pulled out a small bottle of beer.

'For you,' he smiled, as he passed it over. 'You said you like beer.'

What a hero. Where or who he had managed to get alcohol from in the middle of a hospital was anyone's guess. And in the spirit of rebellion that Anatoly had inspired in me, I gladly accepted his present. We watched the football with a camaraderie that often occurs when two people get thrown into an unexpected and stressful situation together. Like being stuck in a broken lift, or being forced to seek shelter in a shop doorway during a sudden and violent rainstorm. The situation breaks down the normal barriers to reveal a human underbelly that disarms both sides, leading to conversations and smiles that would not normally happen. That used to be the case in London (the place I was born and raised) where most suburban homes would have a small patch of garden at the front of the house as well as at the back. It was in that small front garden that you would say hello to your neighbours as they arrived home or nod your head to the regular neighbourhood policeman as he sauntered by. People would mention to the copper that they had seen a strange person loitering on the corner, or that they hadn't seen the old lady Mrs. Smythe from number 82 for a while and did someone need to look in on her? Snippets of information that were more powerful than days of police manpower trying to interrogate suspects. But then with increasing prosperity, everyone decided to pave over their front gardens with concrete, to create 'off-street parking' for their newly acquired vehicles, which in turn increased the value of their properties, especially in a crowded metropolis like London. Suddenly, you no longer had a reason to stand outside and talk to your neighbours or the local bobby. All you saw from then on were screeching squad cars with blue lights flashing as they chased after local yobs, while Mrs. Smythe could be dead and festering for weeks before anyone noticed, and even then, only because of the smell. Camaraderie lost. I had yet to see a front garden anywhere in Moscow, so I surmised that the situation would be even worse here.

As I sat in my hospital bed sipping the beer that Anatoly had brought for me, I wondered if he had ever played football with the German army in the middle of a desperate muddy front-line field in an unlikely pause in fighting, as happened once in an unofficial Christmas truce in the First World War in 1914 – an image often used to denote the folly of war. People in Russia did not like the police, whom they associated with corruption and laziness. But they did have respect for the army, especially the veterans who had defended the country so bravely against Hitler's war machine.

The football match ended and Anatoly fell asleep and began emitting his fulsome trademark snore. As night descended, I looked out at the apartment blocks through the window to my left, watching the lights of different apartments winking on and off, making different patterns to the whole facade as evening turned into night, with eventually only a few remaining on, as darkness enveloped the city. I drifted off…

The next day, I thankfully perked up sufficiently to be able to leave, and eventually made a full recovery. According to a later assessment by a hernia expert in the UK, the Russian surgeon had essentially cut me open like a slab of meat.

'They didn't do anything medically wrong,' he said. 'But let's just say they were a bit robust about it.'

Funnily enough, I would never ever recommend surgery in Russia to anyone – but that's just my experience. Expats, beware. Funny how we Brits who live abroad call ourselves 'expats' while foreign workers who arrive in Britain are referred to as 'immigrants'.

Anyway, by coincidence, Anatoly was also ready to leave the hospital. He barked at his son through his mobile phone, admonishing him for being late to pick him up. Russians do like to have a good shout at each other. On hearing them, you would think that they were all about to have a punch-up, but in fact it was just something about the language that sounded aggressive when really most of the time they were just having a chat, or a friendly dispute. His suitably chastened son eventually arrived and we said our warm goodbyes.

When I got home, I received an email informing me that the previous hospital tests relating to my work contract had all been successful, thus my updated contractual agreement had come through and was ready to be signed. I was to remain in Russia for a while yet. It had already been a roller coaster experience, with unexpected ups and downs, excitement and dangers. Did I want more? Oh, God yes. Especially as finally, and without warning, the

Big Thaw had arrived. As far as I could tell, Russia only had two seasons – the long and tough clenched fist of winter, which had refused to let go for several months, and the short, open-palmed sudden bursting forth of summer. There was nothing in between. It was like someone in the Kremlin had just turned a page and said, 'That was winter, now this is summer,' and the weather did as it was told.

I was going to see the Russians in a different light.

7

STUPID FISH

'In the opinion of all Russians, pigs do not go "Oink, oink"'

The sudden arrival of summer wasn't the only surprise to me; more remarkable was just how hot and humid it had become. Twenty-nine degrees Celsius is not what I had expected in Moscow, but apparently this was actually quite normal for the time of year. It's just that I assumed Russia never had a summer, when in fact it was a darned sight warmer than ours. I even came across a couple of mosquitoes in my apartment – can you believe it? The result of this sunny outlook was a warming of people's attitudes in general. Everyone seemed a lot more friendly and contented, though they didn't so much seem to be enjoying the summer for its own sake – more a case of giving themselves a pat on the back for surviving the odious and interminably long winter. Even the pigeons were waddling around with a greater sense of well-being. At this time of year Russians take to the parks, of which there were a fair few. The most famous is Gorky Park, named after the Soviet writer Maxim Gorky, who was a friend of revolutionary Vladimir Lenin. *Gorky Park* was also the name of a murder thriller set in Moscow. I often mull over the use of the word 'murder' in entertainment shows. *Murder She Wrote* or *Murder on the Orient Express.* Imagine a show or film called *Rape She Wrote* or *Rape on the Orient Express.* That would be an outrage. Yet, the word 'murder'? Yeah, somehow that's okay, which suggests (as vile and unacceptable as rape is) that murder is a less heinous crime. How this has come to be acceptable is a mystery to me.

Anyway, the truth is that Gorky Park, which lies along the banks of the Moscow River, was a shadow of its former self. It was one of those places where the upkeep was not as good as it used to be. Ragged and run-down, it was a strangely sad place, with grey-looking trees scattered around great expanses of weeds rather than grass. There was also a famous funfair there, which again had seen better days, with its creaking, rusty and battered old rides, which looked anything but safe. The funfair workers manned these ancient machines with despair in their eyes and presumably very few roubles in their pockets, as they gazed in a resigned manner at the dwindling number of visitors. These workers were paid very little by the state and they looked so miserable that I started to feel guilty just being there. An odd experience, as if they thought I was mocking them with my very presence – a foreigner who could afford to go to restaurants and bars which in Western terms were not expensive, but which were still completely out of their reach. Their eyes fixed on me as I passed them by, with a distinct feeling of despondency and envy. I did not stay long after that, but instead decided to explore the other green spaces in and around the capital. One of which was near to the Frunzenskaya Metro station, on the south side of the city. Initially the park looked tranquil and well looked after; the perfect place perhaps to relax on the grass with a good book and a little picnic while contemplating life in Moscow. In fact, I even stopped off home on the way, to put a few provisions inside a mini cool box for my small excursion. However, on arrival at the park, which also had a pleasant lake running through the middle, I soon discovered that sitting on the grass was not allowed. As I took my first sip of wine, a stern-looking park warden came up to me, arms waving.

'Nyet!' he bellowed.

God, why does everything in Russia have to be 'No'. He pointed to one of the numerous signs on sticks that had been poked into the grass, warning visitors in Russian not to sit on the greenery. Instead, you were instructed to sit only on the benches provided. To me it seemed that when you have acres of beautiful grass around you, it feels like a prison sentence to be only allowed to park your backside on a mouldy wooden bench, complete with fresh pigeon excrement. Yet as I looked around, I noticed that no one was flouting the law of the park; they were either squashed and huddled on the benches, or standing around waiting for someone to leave, so that they too could be squashed and huddled on a bench. Ludicrous.

I gathered up my things and trundled down to the banks of the lake which had a nice grassy clearing just on the edge. I settled down and again poured myself some wine into a little plastic cup.

'*Nyet!*'

My not-so-friendly neighbourhood warden had followed me down to the water's edge. Clearly, sitting by the water was not allowed either.

'Okay, okay, I'm going!'

This absurdity meant that so far, I had found a horrid park where I didn't want to sit, and a beautiful park where I wasn't *allowed* to sit. How odd. How Russian. There must, I thought, be something else. And indeed, there was. I discovered a huge green space further south, reminiscent of London's sprawling Hampstead Heath, where you could laze around on the grass to your heart's content, surrounded by trees and panoramic views down to the Moscow River, the waterway which bisects the city. I couldn't work out why the rules in this park were different, they just were. In any case, during the few short weeks of warmth in Moscow, it was a welcome break from the tough world of the inner city. I can't say that the air was as clear and fresh as you would expect in a big park and there was a greyness about the foliage on the trees, probably due to the choking pollution from the city's endless standstill traffic. Nevertheless, the Russians around me were enjoying it as much as anyone else. The only difference was their obsession with flowers. The few blossoming trees that were dotted around the area were all surrounded by Russians sampling the aroma from the various blooms. In fact, many girls were having their photos taken next to the flowers. I suppose that the long, hard, dreary winters made any kind of natural colour something to be yearned for and treasured. Not having something can make you more appreciative of it when it finally arrives.

My mobile phone bleeped. It was a message from a friend I had made called Sofia. She was a perky Ukrainian girl with red hair and huge green eyes, whom I'd met in a bar, and who worked in Moscow as a language teacher. She spoke Ukrainian, Russian, Spanish, Hebrew and pretty much perfect English. A phenomenal linguistic feat I thought. And yes, we were just friends. Contrary to what you may be thinking up to this point, due to the revelations thus far of my search for a partner, I do not regard every female I meet as a potential bedmate. No, really.

Text received: Where r you?

Text sent: In a big park somewhere in Moscow.

Text received: Shall I come and meet you? We can have a picnic :)

Text sent: Yes, great :)

This was a very pleasant idea, especially as I already had half a picnic with me, though I decided to bolster my supplies by buying some beer from one of the numerous mobile 'beer kiosks' that seemed to be everywhere in Moscow during summer. Little stalls that would just pop up on the corner of the street or at the pathway crossroads in parks, where you could buy as much beer as you like on tap from little old ladies sitting on wooden stools. They weren't really regulated or sanctioned, but then who didn't want beer in summer? So, the authorities just let most of it happen beneath the radar, much to the delight of summer revellers.

After explaining where I was by describing the layout of the park, Sofia arrived and immediately headed for the nearest flower-adorned tree, asking me to take her photo beneath it. I fished out my phone and obliged.

'It's so nice to be with nature,' she said gleefully.

'Yes,' I replied, looking across the view down to the river. 'Does it have any fish?'

'Maybe,' she replied. 'But fish are stupid.'

This was a good example of a Russian (or in this case a Ukrainian) person saying something completely out of the blue, with no context or explanation.

'Why do you say that?'

'Oh, they just are,' she said matter-of-factly.

I was baffled. It was something I couldn't seem to get to the bottom of – those moments of 'otherness' that would be thrown at you, which you simply could not fathom. For me, it was what made the people of this region different and endearing too. Attractive and frustrating, all at the same time.

I let the 'stupid' fish be and concentrated instead on the other aspects of nature that were all around us. Again, a few pigeons were strutting around on the grass, pecking at the earth for insects and grubs. I often wondered how they managed to see properly. Surely the way their heads bob backwards and forwards on every step makes it impossible to focus on anything for longer than a split second? There was one male pigeon not far from where I was stretched out who was trying to have his wicked way with a female pigeon, in a courtship display that included fanning out his tail feathers whilst trotting towards the pigeon girlie of his choice with a barrage of cooing. She was having none of it, though, and simply flew away, leaving him looking rather embarrassed. I wondered if female Russian pigeons were higher maintenance than Western ones. Maybe they insisted on juicier worms and better quality bedding for the nest before any hanky-panky could commence. Hmmm. But the cooing noises he had been making reminded me of a strange peculiarity of language and culture. From childhood we are all taught the sounds that animals make, right? For example, pigs go, 'Oink, oink' while ducks go, 'Quack, quack'. To me, it's an irrefutable truth, which is obvious to everyone – at least that's what I had imagined. I had made a friend in the form of a girl called Elizaveta. A tall, thirty-something, confident, blue-eyed brunette. She was a translator at my workplace, translating Russian text and words into English for the channel. So she knew what she was talking about when it came to the idiosyncrasies of language. It turned out that in her opinion, and the opinion of all Russians, pigs do not go 'Oink, oink'.

'They go, "Hru, hru,"' she said.

'What do you mean?' I enquired.

'Well, that's how they go,' she said flatly.

I was incredulous, 'Hru, hru?'

'Yes.'

'Well, what about ducks?' I countered.

'They go, "Clack, clack."'

'What? No they don't. They say, "Quack, quack," it's obvious.'

'Don't be silly,' she said, clearly irked.

'Okay, well what about dogs?' I asked, arching my eyebrows.

'Guv, guv.'

'Now that's ridiculous; everyone knows they go, "Woof, woof."'

She looked at me like a teacher about to admonish an errant pupil who had not done his homework.

'Look,' she said. 'Russians don't always know how to say the sound that comes with the letter "w". So they can't say "q-w-uack" or "o-w-ink" or "woof". It's just not a sound used in the Russian language. And anyway, you're just wrong.'

'Oh, I see,' I said sheepishly.

Elizaveta was old enough to remember what it was like to live through Soviet times, when no one was allowed out of the country and no one was allowed in. When there were hardly any shops, with hardly any produce. Russians' understanding of the rest of the world was like looking through a tiny hole in a wall – they could just about make out a magical colourful place on the other side, but were always wary that too much time spent looking through the hole could get you into trouble. Ordinary people could only get a glimpse of what we in the West took for granted. At her school, pupils would gather around the kids who had rich parents. Not for any kind of kudos, but simply the fact that those kids would, every now and then, bring in wondrous fragments from the outside world, given to them by their diplomat parents who had just returned from some trip or other. A music cassette of Duran Duran, a scratchy VHS video of *Top Gun*, or a digital calculator. As a result, these things became hugely popular in the Soviet Union, albeit in total secrecy. Every note, every image and every gadget would be pored over by a population who had been fed from birth with a diet of only officially sanctioned patriotic Soviet doctrine and rubbish technology. I had recently been to see the pop star Seal on tour at a venue in Moscow, and what was most surprising to me was how everyone knew the lyrics to all his songs. I imagined how all the Russians in the audience had as kids huddled around a creaking old cassette player to listen to 'Kiss from a Rose' again, and again, and again...

Of course, these snippets of another world often led to a misleading impression that life was all fun and games in the West, and indeed when the Berlin Wall came down, the East Germans soon had to get used to strange new concepts like unemployment, street crime, competition, high transport costs, soaring heating bills, the list goes on – in short, capitalism. I am sure they would say that the price was worth paying in order to live a life without fear of censorship, or worse. But I had to say it seemed that most Russians still had a somewhat rose-tinted view of the West. Either way, it was still a challenge and a surprise to discover that historical events I took for granted had hardly touched the lives of other people who were living on the same planet. Similarly, what did we in the West know about the daily lives of people living in this part of the former Soviet Union? Not a lot. What we do hear about, though, is a relentless Western media narrative of how authoritarian the alternating Russian leader Vladimir Putin is. Squashing any opposition, not allowing real democracy, still using his former KGB contacts to muscle out any dissent, and allowing his bloated oligarch friends to do more or less what they want. Yet, at the same time we fail to understand the extent to which the majority of the population are still very much in favour of him. Elizaveta told me how during the nineties when the alcoholic President Boris Yeltsin was supposed to have been in charge, there was complete chaos in the streets. For while he danced red-nosed and inebriated during televised public events, there were gangs, shootings, mafia and complete lawlessness and fear on the ground. She and her friends were afraid to go out at night. One evening, she went out for a drink with a female friend, and suddenly a boorish guy at the bar turned to them.

'You two, stay here, you are with me for the night.'

There was real menace in his voice, and the look on the face of the barman said that if they had refused to obey, they would be physically attacked, if not murdered. Clearly some kind of gang leader. Luckily, he got so drunk he forgot about them, and they were able to slip away. But it was a close call, and for years they rarely ventured out again. Putin's rise to power brought the one thing which the Russians revere above all else – stability. Sure, they don't like corruption, or lack of choice, or bureaucracy, or backward infrastructure, but none of those failings seem to overtake that one state of being they crave more than anything else. And Putin knew it from the start. Elizaveta hated all the bad things about her country, but at least she could go out in the evening in relative safety. This was not to say that she didn't crave all the good things from the West as well, it's just that the spectre of instability haunts the Russian psyche like nothing else. This may change of course, as a younger, internet-savvy generation, untouched by events in the 1990s, wonder why it is they have to live in a place which only grudgingly allows any kind of dissent. In the run-up to any large protest in Moscow, for example, Metro stations around the edge of the city are mysteriously closed for 'maintenance work' while thousands of cars coming into the capital are stopped and turned back due to 'motoring irregularities'. Anything to keep the numbers down. But here's a philosophical question: How does a leader hold a country together as large as Russia for any length of time, without some form of authoritarianism? Arguably, the answer is, you can't. I am not for one second advocating this of course; the horrors of dictatorship are well documented down the years. I am just wondering what, ideologically, the alternatives are. After all, I don't much remember the British Empire being particularly partial to democracy in India, for example – the foreign governors living off the fat of the land while millions of Indians died of famine. In the end, the bloated excesses of colonialism, and the sheer unmanageable scale of it, came tumbling down, and change happened. Would change happen in Russia? Would it need to? And if it did, who's to say it should be the kind of change that we in the West regard as acceptable?

I was ruminating on these matters as Sofia and I lay on the welcoming green grass of the Moscow park we were in, observing the Russians going to and fro, eating their ice creams and drinking their beers, bantering and generally having fun, in a way which perhaps they would not have been able to a couple of decades back. There's something about relaxing in an open space which has a way of clearing your mind and giving you time to think about things away from the restrictive routine of daily life. As the sun eventually began to set, we gathered up the remnants of our picnic and headed back to our respective homes. She was a good soul, Sofia. Just before we parted, I bought her some flowers from a stall outside the Metro station. She liked that and went happily on her way.

The tranquillity of the day reminded me of another rare place of greenery within the city boundaries – the one and only golf course that was anywhere near the centre of town. Now golf had only recently arrived in Russia. It is, of course, a sport which epitomises wealth, privilege and general snottiness. What makes me laugh are all the golfers in the world who say stuff like, 'Oh, it's a noble sport which demands courtesy, good manners and an understanding of comradeship and graciousness in defeat, unlike other sports.' Bollocks. The number of golfers who cheat is phenomenal. Suddenly 'finding' a ball when it is supposed to be lost in the bushes (dropping a hidden one from their pocket) or pretending to be a far worse player than you really are, so that you get an easier ranking in a more important match to come, or coughing to distract your opponent as they are about to take a shot. The list of malpractice and skulduggery in golf is endless. Speaking of which, the furore over Tiger Woods' various extramarital affairs was regarded by Russians as quite ridiculous. His televised apologies to his advertising sponsors for his behaviour were met with howls of incredulity in bars across Moscow. Their reasoning was, 'Are we really saying that every single chairman and director in the boardrooms of top Western advertising companies have never ever had an affair? *Really?* What with their fat expense accounts and paid-for trips to exotic locations on big yachts, with the weight of booze and prostitutes almost sinking the boat itself? Are we really saying that Western advertising executives are the custodians of society's moral compass?' One of my Russian colleagues told me how he had been invited to a prestigious golf event held near Moscow a couple of years back. He related how on his way out of the event he noticed a whole coachload of very glamorous Russian women being bussed in to the hotel where all the golfers were staying. Naively, he asked his taxi driver if there was to be a women's tournament held there as well? The taxi driver just laughed and replied, 'No, those girls are for tonight's party.' And there you have it. He told me that a couple of the people who were quick to criticise Tiger Woods for his many (reprehensible) indiscretions were themselves present at that very party and had spent the evening scoring more than a few birdies. The hypocrisy speaks for itself.

Anyway, the sun was most definitely shining this month and the Russians were at play. Walking in parks, playing golf, eating ice lollies, jumping into lakes, and any other outdoor activity they could get their hands on. *Shashlik* was another one. It's their word for skewers of lamb in particular, or any other meat being barbecued over hot coals. Everyone had their own special recipe for the marinade, which resulted in an endless form of Russian social debate, with the *shashlik* being the centre of attention. And damn nice it tasted too. Just as well really, as the rest of the year Russian food was pretty bland to say the least. But this was the month for outdoor living, with many Russians owning a country house, or *dacha* out in the suburbs of Moscow, normally about one or two hours' journey away by car. This would be a second home, for those who could afford it, to get away from the stresses and choking pollution of the city. On a Friday night, the roads out of Moscow would be crammed with people escaping to their *dachas*, their cars full of food shopping for their weekend getaway. In the UK, most homes in the country look more or less in keeping with each other. You might see an old village full of homes with thatched roofs, or perhaps a town full of Georgian architecture. But in Russia, anything goes. The moment you leave the outer ring road and the bland concrete suburbs, the flat grassy scenery becomes dotted with the oddest shaped buildings, made of all manner of different materials – wood, stone, plastic, bricks and who knows what else. Like some mad architect who had been given free reign to design whatever nonsense had just popped into his or her head. And the colours too – red houses, green, blue, white, almost anything seemed to be acceptable, with each house surrounded by a plot of land about two or three times the size of the building. Clearly very lax planning regulations, if any. I was viewing all of this from the passenger seat of my regular taxi driver's car. Anton (the fellow who had picked me up from the airport on my first day in Russia) had unexpectedly invited me to spend a day at his *dacha* – a kind of 'thank you' for being a regular customer I suppose. Anton's country retreat turned out to be a three-storey wooden pine affair, with a massive triangular roof. The roof itself was about twice as big as the rest of the house, as he had basically decided to build upwards and given that he liked triangles, it seemed the right thing to do. He had even had some triangular windows installed too. No one had ever complained, so the triangles stayed. The house was surrounded by a big plot of land, on which he and his wife were growing strawberries, tomatoes, cucumbers, pumpkins, onions and herbs. There were cherry trees, apples, raspberries and plums too. He had constructed a greenhouse, a carport, and the biggest garden shed I had ever seen in which to store every possible tool known to mankind. Russians threw nothing away, because they never knew when something could be useful in the future and good materials and tools were expensive and hard to come by. The monster shed on its own was bigger than the average two-up, two-down house in the UK, and full to the brim of anything he had been able to get his hands on.

'Cary, this my chainsaw. And this my hedge trimmer, and this small tool for wood carving, and here my screwdrivers, and here old car engine, and here I have old Soviet suitcase...'

It was extraordinary. The house itself was a maze of unfinished rooms, with bits of wood, screws, hardboard, bottles, sandpaper, old clothes, an old radiator, tins… just anything, everywhere. And yet, in all this jumble, he was gradually making progress. Hiring workers was not cheap, and buying materials was a piecemeal affair, only possible when one could afford it, so Anton had hit upon an idea. His worker, a short, stocky, dark-haired Ukrainian man called Alexander, actually lived at the house, with his wife Tatiana. Two live-in workers. This was not as daft an idea as it first seemed. With the house in such a state of transition and building materials all over the place, it was useful to have someone there for security purposes if nothing else. So when Anton and his wife Irina arrived for a weekend away from the city, they would all four just have lunch and dinner together, as though Alexander and Tatiana were part of the family. The latter pair didn't have a house of their own in Russia and were unemployed, so it worked out to the benefit of all concerned. And Anton had been renovating this house for twelve years. Yes, twelve *years*. As far as I could see, it would turn out to be a lifetime project, but one which he was enjoying nonetheless.

His daughter was also there. A thoughtful sixteen-year-old who was studying hard at school and aiming to go to university first in Russia, and then maybe abroad. Her English was impeccable and her ambition more than apparent. She and her contemporaries would be the future of this vast land, and I wondered if constructing a *dacha* for twelve years would be on the agenda for her future life, or whether instead she would want to fly away to some foreign place to experience a more international existence.

While the girls started cooking in the kitchen, us boys went off to the back of the land where Anton had constructed his own *banya*. But not like a small room of the sort you get in a health club. I mean a sauna the size of a small house. Two storeys high, with a changing area, tea and TV zone, shower room, dining table; the works. The three of us stripped off and went to sit in the scorching sauna, dressed only in silly-looking triangular felt hats, designed to protect your brain from the effects of the heat. It was then that Anton gestured to Alexander.

'He military man, he fight in Afghanistan.'

I looked at Alexander. He shrugged his shoulders with a nonchalant look on his face.

'Yes, two years. I drive army trucks.'

Two years in the nine-year Soviet war against the Mujahideen, the radical Islamists of the 1980s. When you meet someone who says he was in the army, the only question you really want to ask is, 'Did you kill anyone?' And yet it's also the last question you are able to force from your lips, always worried that it's too personal a question, or one which could change the atmosphere in the room, or maybe you think that whoever you are asking will suddenly fly off into a Rambo-style rage with uncontrollable flashbacks of terrible moments in the war, and before you know it he'll be slitting your throat with a piece of hot coal from the sauna oven, while not even flinching from the searing rock that is burning his own flesh. And so I didn't ask, and to be honest he did not seem that keen to discuss his experiences, so who was I to intrude upon his trauma? Alexander reached for a metal ladle, scooped up some water from a wooden bucket and poured it over the coals. The heat was stupendous, and this time (unlike my previous *banya* experience) I stuck it out and succumbed to being whipped on my back with bunches of branches and leaves. Alexander went at it with wild abandon while I hoped he wasn't reliving some kind of wartime torture routine.

Swish! Swish! Swish!

Anton was laughing his head off as I howled in pain.

'It is good for skin,' he smiled.

Eventually the skin care regime was over and I staggered out of the sauna for the welcome relief of a more comfortable temperature in the tearoom. We sat with cups of tea, lemon and sugar, and smoked some kind of fruity stuff from an Egyptian hookah, one of those contraptions with a bulb of water at the base and some mouth pipes rising from the middle. We changed and went back to join the girls for a Russian feast. They had barbecued a huge salmon and presented it with some traditional Russian fare – potatoes, homemade black bread, a cucumber yoghurt thing mixed with dill, and a sweet onion dish, all of which was actually rather tasty.

'You've done a great job with your *dacha*, Anton.'

'Thank you,' he shrugged.

I looked around at the work in progress.

'But when will it be finished?'

Again, the Russian shrug of the shoulders.

'I don't know.'

Like many aspects of Russia, time and the completion of a project was not of the essence. For them, the journey was just as rewarding as the end product and in any case most people did not have the resources to do it any other way.

On the journey back into town from Anton's *dacha*, we drove along a bridge over the Moscow River, and indeed one of the highlights of the month was to be a boat trip along the winding stretch of water itself, which divides the city in two.

I had been invited by George, the socialite to beat all socialites, who had accordingly summoned half of Moscow to join him on a river cruise. He was one of those people that seemed to need people around him, as if fearing that without their acknowledgement of his existence, he would simply disappear. The boat was moored up on the banks of the river near the Hotel Ukraina, and we all piled onto its decks during one gloriously sunny afternoon. Now this was something the Russians did well. The boat was a two-deck cruiser, with the bottom deck encased in a glass canopy so you could see everything from your posh white cloth-covered table; a complete wraparound view. There was a band playing at one end, a bar dispensing drinks at the other, and a load of waiters and waitresses flitting around taking food and drink orders. Then there was the upper deck that was open to the elements – a perfect spot to take photos of the Kremlin and the colourful 'onion building' as we foreigners called it (Saint Basil's Cathedral is its proper name, but all the turrets look like huge onions). George was one of those optimists who believed everyone was nice unless proven otherwise, whereas I tended to be the opposite – that way, you are never disappointed, but only pleasantly surprised. Either way, the group he had invited were an interesting mix of foreigners, Russians, liberals, not-so liberals and some oddballs too. There was one middle-aged Russian woman who had come with her English husband, yet seemed to spend most of the time staring meaningfully at me right under her husband's nose, who didn't seem to notice. Either that, or he was getting some kind of kick out of it. I kept getting the feeling she was going to molest me at any moment, and when she somehow managed to spill some wine on the cuff of my shirt 'by mistake', I quickly made an excuse about having to go to the toilet (and I thought only women used that excuse) before she could get any further with the, 'Let me help you clean up your shirt' routine. Then there was a beautiful Russian woman who turned out to be the daughter of a retired KGB agent. All the while she was talking to me, I kept wondering if perhaps her dad had hidden a secret camera on one of the oversized diamond rings she was wearing, which was busy snapping photos of me as she held her glass of wine. Probably just paranoia. I went to stand on the top deck, taking in the sights as we sailed on down the river, the sun overhead, drink in hand, Russian music and revelry wafting up from the deck below. What a great scene. The red-brick walls of the Kremlin drifted by as did the huge and ungainly statue of Peter the Great, a dreadful piece of metallic art perched on a kind of jetty, depicting an oversized Peter gesturing skywards atop a boat. Nearly a hundred metres high, it was so ugly the local authorities in Moscow had actually tried to give it away to the northern city of Saint Petersburg, but the authorities there had politely declined. It was created by a Georgian-Russian sculptor by the name of Tsereteli, a self-proclaimed artist who, due to his reportedly close associations with the hierarchy, had apparently received pot-loads of money to create massive, and in my opinion, frighteningly crap works of sculpted art. He even had his own gallery space to store and display these monstrosities, and just like the emperor's new clothes, no one ever said anything publicly about the nonsense he created. Even I, bereft of artistic knowledge, could appreciate how truly awful they were. He had admittedly created one decent one, depicting Franklin D. Roosevelt, Winston Churchill and Joseph Stalin all sitting side by side at the Yalta Conference in Crimea in early 1945, where Roosevelt pretended he didn't think Stalin was a boorish oaf, and Churchill pretended he actually had a say when it came to carving up Europe after the Second World War. I think Tsereteli should have left it at that and quit while he was ahead.

The boat continued on its journey, passing the British Embassy (a strangely out of place modern glass and steel box of a building), Christ the Saviour Cathedral (head office of the Orthodox Church in Russia; they of the long beards and fat bank accounts) and the Red October Chocolate Factory. The latter were chocolate makers to the Tsars, whose headquarters had become something of a national symbol down the years, with its imposing red-brick facade and copious production of sweet treats loved by Russians young and old.

The river trip was nearing its end. Little did I know that the heat of the last few weeks was about to mutate from a very pleasant summer to a ferocious incarnation that was to be downright life-threatening.

8

FIRE AND GRIMSTONE

'Maybe it was an evil premonition of some kind'

It must have been a nightmare. Or was it? The weird thing was, I hadn't fallen asleep. I was lying there in the dark in my bed, feeling tired, when suddenly I felt that someone or some*thing* was holding me down. I knew I wasn't asleep, because my eyes were open and I could see the outline of the bedside table – I just couldn't move, as hard as I tried. Some kind of 'entity' was physically holding my back and neck down onto the bed, and I was scared. It went on for what seemed about a minute, until finally, whatever it was left the room and I was able to leap up, turn on the bedside lamp and take deep breaths of relief and terror all mixed up. Yes, it sounds ridiculous, and of course psychologists have devised an explanation for this frightening phenomenon.

They say that if you are particularly stressed, your mind refuses to let you sleep, because you are so preoccupied with whatever predicament you feel you are in. Maybe you are worried about your job, or your relationship, or an impending interview and so on. But at the same time, your body still needs to shut down for a while to allow you to sleep. As a result, part of your brain does this for you whether you like it or not, while at the same time another part of your brain is still consciously functioning. Hence, the feeling of being 'held down' is simply your body going into shutdown, while part of you is still aware of being awake – eyes open, looking at things and so forth. It all sounds very plausible doesn't it? But I can guarantee that when it's happening, it just feels like there's some kind of goblin on your back. Maybe it was an evil premonition of some kind. Difficult to square with my non-religious, non-goblin views, but who knows? I went to the kitchen for a glass of water. There seemed to be an odd smell in the air, like something was burning, but I hadn't used the cooker or the toaster for at least a couple of days. I went to the window. Darkness outside. No towering inferno to be seen, and no commotion from any of the neighbours. I went back to bed. When I eventually woke up, everything had changed.

Not many people outside Russia realise that Moscow has one of the hottest summers in the Northern Hemisphere. Somehow it doesn't fit into the normal cliché of unending blizzards and piles of snow. Yet T-shirts, barbecues and outdoor swimming pools are as normal in Russia during the summer as constant drizzling rain is in Manchester (as a student, I lived in Manchester for four years and as far as I remember, it rained nearly every day). So the soaring temperatures were a welcome few weeks of fun and frolics for a population who yearn for a bit of sunshine on their sun-starved faces. A time to unwind with their friends without the constant worry of slipping over on the ice. A time to forget their troubles. A time to feel happy to be alive. Nearly every street café or restaurant had built itself a temporary veranda in front of their eateries for customers to sit outside in the shade, sip their beers and watch the world go by. But this summer was to be different. This summer would test the people's resolve to the limit. It had all started so well, with several carefree days of warmth and jollity. Everyone was in a good mood, smiling, laughing and enjoying life. But the night I had woken up (or not fallen asleep) with the beast on my back, had by morning turned into something a lot more than just a strange whiff. At first, I and everyone else assumed it was people having illegal barbecues; having a crafty grill on your apartment balcony was not allowed, as you could easily set the whole building on fire. But in any case, it wasn't really the smell of a burning sausage or smouldering burger, it was more the smell of... well... just burning. Maybe a local factory had succumbed to a blaze? But it would have to have been one heck of a fire, as everyone across Moscow could smell it. As it turned out, it *was* one heck of a fire, but bigger than anyone could have imagined. You see, Moscow is surrounded by miles and miles of peat bogs, or at least it once was. Peat is basically rotten vegetation that sits on top of, or below, marshy areas. There's a lot of it in Scotland, for example, where over the centuries people would dig it up, dry it out, and use it to light domestic fires. Left underground long enough, peat eventually turns into coal. The trouble was that in Russia, the water in the bogs had been drained during the 1960s in order to harvest the peat, to use as fuel in electricity power stations and to make way for agriculture. In other words, those areas still had the peat, but without the bogs. Perfect fuel to create electricity, but even more perfect fuel for an angry wildfire. Of course, the climate in and around Moscow was never quite hot enough to put this to the test… until now. The city's population was enduring one of the hottest and driest summers ever seen, and sure enough the peat around the city caught fire, and then some. When you think of a big fire, you tend to imagine that you can just turn on your hosepipe and douse it in a couple of minutes. But as with most things concerning the environment, we humans fail to comprehend the overwhelming power of Mother Nature. When a wall of fire ten metres high is coming towards you fanned by high-speed winds, believe me there's no time to turn on your hosepipe. You just have to run for your life and hope that the wind changes direction. The fires around Moscow caught everyone by surprise, not least the State Fire Service which had been underfunded and ill-prepared for anything like this. They vainly dispatched motley crews here or there, with no planning, no strategy and often no water, just people in ragged uniforms trying to put the flames out with sand and spades. Then there was the nature of the peat bog, in that many of the fires were *underground*, meaning the fire crews didn't quite know where the flames would pop up next, a bit like that fairground whack-a-mole game where you bash the critter on the head, only to see it pop up out of another hole. The result of all this? A smoke cloud to rival all smoke clouds. The wind then fanned this smoke precisely over Moscow, to completely cover the city in dense, choking smog. There was no sunshine and you could not see further than two metres in front of you. It was like being inside a burning building, but with no way out. The smoke seared itself into my lungs, and I was starting to feel a sense of panic. The first thing most people did was to duck into air-conditioned shopping centres. The centres simply filled up with people who were not there to shop, but just to breathe. The DIY shops which were packed with desperate throngs trying to buy builders' masks, had all sold out within a couple of hours. This too being a place of limited commercial nous, there were no plans to bring in or produce any more masks over and above the allotted amount that had already been sent to the shops. Pretty soon though, officials at the shopping centres were telling everyone to get out; as far as they were concerned all these squatters were just clogging up any legitimate trade, ignoring the fact that this was something of a major emergency. Even a Metro journey was a trial in itself, as the system was full of smoke, with desperate commuters holding handkerchiefs up to their mouths as the fumes stung their red-raw eyes. And for the majority of the city's population, getting home offered little relief. Most apartments did not have air conditioning. 'Why not just close the windows?' I hear you ask. Well, when the temperature is nearing 40 degrees Celsius, if you closed all your windows, you would literally bake inside. But if you opened the windows, you would die of smoke inhalation. It was like a choice offered by some crazy murderous waiter.

'How would you like your death sir, baked or smoked?'

And die, people did. This was a serious situation, to which there seemed no serious response. The then Mayor of Moscow was nowhere to be seen, as he was holidaying at the time and seemed in no hurry to return to deal with the situation (his hesitancy eventually cost him his job). Thousands of people stayed at work as long as they could, not because they fancied putting in a load of overtime, but because most workplaces had air conditioning units. It was a case of work and breathe or go home and suffocate. Ironically, you would still see little huddles of workers around the side of buildings having their cigarette breaks – as if their lungs hadn't suffered enough already.

There was an eerie atmosphere across the city. The smog hung around like the set of some old horror film, impossibly thick and refusing to budge no matter what, fuelled by the peat bog blazes outside the city. This was fire and brimstone all right. People were praying for rain, which refused to come, and until it did there was a feeling of helplessness and real anger against the authorities, which were perceived to be not doing very much. Various heads would roll of course, but the damage this was doing to the image of Moscow as a modern city was immense. The tourists could not believe their smoky eyes. Meanwhile, foreign companies that had outposts in Moscow actually told their employees to get the next flight out of the city, as the airports were still (inexplicably) working. Everyone else? Well, they just had to suffer. The trick was to find somewhere, anywhere, that had air conditioning. For a while, the cinemas did a roaring trade, packed to capacity with gasping Russians, preferring to endure even for just a couple of hours the latest overhyped and badly directed Hollywood blockbuster, than choke to death in the streets. Myself, I was fortunate enough to have air conditioning at my pad. I sat on my sofa watching the images right outside my apartment making news around the world, as people filmed the blanket of vile smog on their smartphones and pinged the pictures around the globe. Russians had developed an obsession with anything to do with communication, especially Facebook, which to be honest I was never a big fan of. Why? Well, it's the way addicted Facebook users look at you when you answer their presumptuous question. It goes like this:

'Are you on Facebook?'

'No.'

'You're not on Facebook?'

'No, I'm not.'

'What, you mean you're not on Facebook?'

'That's right, I'm not on Facebook.'

(Look of confusion).

'Why not?'

'Because, at this stage of humanity's development, as far as I'm aware, I still have a choice. And I choose not to be.'

They then look at you as if you have just said, 'I believe in witchcraft and the all-encompassing evil power of the almighty wizard-master. He shall reign supreme and eat your children.'

It's just the disdain that one attracts by being different that irks me. Free speech and free thought, remember that? I remember meeting up with a friend once who spent more time taking photos of nothing in particular and sending them to her online 'friends' than actually having a face-to-face conversation with me. Every time I began a sentence, her phone would beep and she would turn away to reply to someone's 'like'. It was as if she had an attention-seeking child in her pocket. At least the Russians had an excuse. They had lived through decades of being suppressed in terms of communicating with the outside world, so had a voracious appetite for gadgetry. Hence, every Russian had, or wanted to have, a smartphone. Sadly though, I began to notice the West's penchant for unnecessary technology seeping through to Russian culture too. In one air-conditioned bar I had ducked into the day before, I saw a group of six young Russian guys and girls sitting around a table, with drinks and food being served periodically to them. Yet they were not talking to each other. Not one word. Instead, they were each glued to their devices – texting, typing, liking, poking, prodding, farting… all the things that people seem to spend most of their waking time doing on their mobiles these days. An ostensible show of communication, yet ironically nothing much of actual value to say. And the Russians had caught the bug. Text, text, text. Tweet, tweet, tweet. If you took one of their phones away, they would look at you as if it were some kind of life-support machine. 'Pleeeease give it back! If I don't tweet something in the next two minutes, I'm going to die!' they'd implore. One internet social network survey famously discovered that around forty per cent of social media communications at any one time can be described as 'pointless babble'. Exactly my point. 'But haven't you used social media to promote your book?' I hear people say. That's like asking, 'Have you driven your horribly polluting car to work, when there was no alternative public transport available?' What choice does one have?

So anyway, the Russian smoke-out was seen all over the world, much to the embarrassment of the authorities. This disastrous state of affairs continued all month. Eventually, after what seemed like an eternity, the rains came and did the job which the humans had failed to do, namely put out the fires and dampen down the smoke. It had been a sobering experience. We think we control the earth with our phones, our satellites, our GPS systems, our tablet computers... but in fact we are just ants drifting around on random bits of wood, floating haphazardly in a vast ocean. The natural world can strike us down whenever it wishes, and nobody, not even in the biggest country on the planet, can do anything about it.

So pretty soon Moscow was back to... well... its normal level of pollution. Strange how breathing several cubic metres of car exhaust each day can seem a welcome relief compared to what we had just endured. It's all relative isn't it? I decided then that perhaps it was time to explore a little further afield and get out of the metropolis for a while. I had often been told that Moscow was 'not Russia' and that outside the confines of the city was a vast country that was much the same as it had been during the years of stagnation behind the Iron Curtain. That being the case, it was time to leave my relative comfort zone and see where my nose led me, in order to get another perspective of Moscow – this time from the outside. First stop, a trip to a place that used to be part of the Soviet Union, but had gone its own way. A country where tensions were high between those who saw their future in the West and those who pined for the old-style certainties of a state-controlled society. A land which, in the search for that elusive long-term partner, could well turn out to be my Shangri-La.

Ukraine, here I come.

9

FROM THE OUTSIDE, LOOKING IN

'Puking in the toilets? Oh, yes.'

September was to be a month of travel, starting with Ukraine. Or is it *the* Ukraine? As a linguistics teacher, Sofia had once asked me why Westerners say 'the' in front of her native country's name. I surmised that maybe we were used to using the word 'the' in front of UK, and that any country that started with the letter 'U' would similarly have to be preceded by a 'the'. She thought about this for a moment.

'But you don't say 'the' Uruguay, do you?'

This was a good point, to which I had no answer. Anyway, a trip to (the) Ukraine. Or that had been the plan, until after some thought I decided upon a postponement, in favour of a brief trip back to the UK first. Ukraine would have to wait. That might sound ridiculous in terms of enlightening you about Russia, but as it turned out, my short visit to Blighty would reveal a lot more about Russia, and indeed about myself, than I had expected. It was also to be my first trip away since I had arrived in Russia what seemed ages ago, on that snowy airport tarmac. I just thought I needed a break from the intensity of my experiences in Moscow and imagined that a shot of good old-fashioned British home comforts would be just the ticket.

I had decided to travel with the Russian airline Aeroflot, or 'Aeroflop' as it was rather disparagingly known in the West, due mainly to its shockingly poor past safety record. I'll say this though – nowadays the planes leave on time, arrive on time, and the staff are friendly and efficient. Plus, I haven't had any accidents in one either; that's good enough for me. Sitting in my aisle seat and watching the Russians come on board, I couldn't help noticing the tall, drop-dead killer babe who was ambling towards me with her bags. I wondered where she would end up sitting. She stopped right next to my aisle and motioned to the empty seat to my left. Next to me! A late twenties, curvaceous, pouting, hot pants-wearing wet dream of a girl, all legs, perfume, high heels and lipstick, simply dripping in jewellery, Gucci bags and diamond-encrusted iPhones. I glanced in her direction. Not a flicker of response from her and I wondered if I should try to strike up a conversation. But then I thought… this ostentatious display of designer labels and perfections, tailored sexiness and poise, gemstones and accessories. In Moscow, that was likely to mean one thing – she was being 'sponsored' by someone. Maybe her Russian oligarch boyfriend, who was waiting in his newly acquired mansion in Highgate, or some equally rich British playboy who had long since forgotten the distinction between prostitution and a relationship – tainted as he had become by the trappings and laziness of wealth and desire. Was this the kind of pairing that I was going to be subjected to in Russia? I was no millionaire, but this 'you can shag me as long as you can keep me in Jimmy Choo shoes' relationship contract, seemingly so prevalent in Moscow, was not what I had in mind. She also had the most ridiculously oversized and garish white and gold handbag. I stopped ogling for a moment and looked around the cabin. As far as I could tell, you could take basically anything you wanted as hand luggage on Russian planes, and many of these Russians had suitcases which were well over what was acceptable on other airlines in terms of size and weight. They'd also brought on board trolley-loads of booze (were they going to open them during the flight?) and I counted two miniature dogs and a cat – their owners strapping nappies onto the hapless creatures in case they did a poo during the flight. Surely these animals wouldn't make it through passport control in the UK? I wondered if their owners had been charged a 'moggy and pooch rate' for their pets' seats. A very relaxed attitude all round then; perhaps a bit too relaxed at times, with a good proportion of the Russian men drunk on vodka within the first hour of the flight (alas, they did open those trolleys of booze) all gathering at the back near to the toilets where they began to shout at each other in merriment and drink themselves senseless. Puking in the toilets? Oh, yes. The poor flight attendants clearly had no authority to stop all this from happening. In Moscow, rank had its privileges, and this plane was technically still part of the city's cultural and legal jurisdiction, albeit on a long airborne string, and these guys were clearly 'connected' in some way. I turned and watched these oafs retching all over the place, laughing at their own idiocy as the drinking continued unabated. Horrible. And yet in some ways I much preferred all this (minus the vomiting) to flights on UK airlines, with their endless safety announcements and busybody crew. And that was what I noticed most about returning to London; it had turned into a 'health and safety' nightmare.

'Stand well away from the doors, sir...'

'Move back behind the yellow line, sir...'

'Queue on that side, sir...'

'Don't lean on the glass, sir...'

'Seat belts must be worn on this coach, sir...'

'Do not attempt to zip up your trousers before tucking away your penis, sir it can be dangerous for your health and safety...'

But coming from Moscow where you can do basically anything you like (except sit on the grass in selected parks), London was a rather unpleasant shock. The endless announcements. The small-minded, petty, so-called security people with their fluorescent yellow jackets and supercilious attitude – all wannabe police officers who never made it into the force due to their basic stupidity. Contemptible spineless dullards whose only aim in life is to make your life more miserable than theirs. And 'health and safety' has given them the perfect opportunity to do so.

'Why can't I stand over here?'

'Health and safety, sir.'

'Why can't I queue over there?'

'Health and safety, sir.'

'Why can't I walk over the yellow line?'

'Health and safety, sir.'

'Why can't I take this seat belt, wrap it around your scrawny neck and squeeze it until your weasel eyes pop out of your stupid head?'

'Removing the seat belt would contravene health and safety, sir...'

In Moscow, if you try to cross the road when the red man is showing and you get squashed by a car, well too bad. If you fall off a terrace because you knowingly walked too near to the edge, well too bad. No court case, no ridiculous claim for compensation. Just a Russian shrug of the shoulders. Got caught spraying graffiti on the walls of the Moscow Metro? Expect a good kicking from the police and a fine for wasting police time. Brilliant.

Anyway, back in Britain, I went to visit a friend in the town of Royal Wootton Bassett in Wiltshire. I have to say that a good pint of beer, ordered in English, a good hearty Sunday roast and a good dose of country hospitality was a complete tonic. I had not realised just how much low-level stress I had been living with in Russia by not knowing the language, not understanding signs and directions, being constantly stared at and not being totally at ease with the culture. As extraordinary as the experience had been thus far, it had also worn me down to some extent, both mentally and physically. I went to do some shopping in town. Again, the experience of seeing things that I knew and understood – familiar shop names, friendly service, decent food. I then decided to get some money out of a cash point, but let me first explain the background to that simple statement of intent. My wages from RT were paid monthly into my Russian bank account. However, I needed periodically to transfer some of that money into my still existing UK account, as I wasn't one hundred per cent content with leaving all my money in Russia – during the 1990s there had been a financial crash in the country leading to the value of the currency plummeting. However, transferring money electronically from a Russian account to a UK one had proved almost impossible, as no one in the bank spoke English, all the paperwork had to be filled in by you in Russian, and the fees for the transaction were exorbitant (up to one hundred pounds per transfer!) – in short, they didn't want you to. The rouble was a weak currency, so they wanted to keep the money in, as opposed to letting it out. 'Why not just carry cash on the plane?' I hear you ask. Well, that too had been clamped down on, as the authorities had imposed a strict maximum on how much you could physically take in your pockets. So, after much trial and error, all the British expats working in Russia had hit upon a way of getting around this problem (stay with me, you'll see where I'm going with this in a minute). They discovered that if they went to the UK (which many did periodically to see friends and family) they could simply use their Russian bank cards in a UK cash machine to take out their Russian wages in pounds sterling, incurring only a small charge! Da-da!

All of this resulted in expats running around the UK taking out vast wads of money from cash points. This is not to say that they were stinking rich or anything, they just needed to pay for mortgages, put money into savings, leave some money for their families etc., all of which had to be taken out in one go, while they were still on a short trip to the UK. One colleague was using this perfectly legitimate method of taking out what was, after all, his own money, from a cash point in a street in north London. When he got home, he began counting it all out on his kitchen table, putting it into neat little piles. Suddenly, there was a knock on his front door. He went to open it to find two policemen standing on his porch.

'Good morning sir, we're from the Metropolitan Police; we observed you taking out an unusual quantity of monies from a cash dispensing machine in the last hour. May we come in?' said one of the officers.

With some bemusement, he let them in. Immediately, one of the officers spotted the piles of cash on the table.

'May we ask how you came to be in possession of this quantity of currency, sir?'

'I got it in Russia.'

'Oh *really*, sir, perhaps we ought to go for a chat down the station...'

'No, no, you don't understand! It's just my wages, because...'

'Come along now, sir, we don't want to cause any trouble, do we…?'

After showing him his business card, passport, work permit and other documents, he finally persuaded the officers that he was not a drug dealer or a money launderer. But it was a close thing. I too was about to experience the hand of suspicion as I stood in front of the cash machine in Wootton Bassett high street. I keyed in my pass code, and the fresh notes came rolling out. I then went into the bank, filled in the form, and asked the cashier to put it into my UK account. A simple procedure, right? Wrong.

'Oh, these are nice crispy notes, sir,' she said, raising her eyebrows.

'Er… well, yes, I suppose they are,' I stammered.

She began thumbing through them before putting them onto the counting machine.

'You've got quite a lot, haven't you?'

This was unbelievable. What a cheek. I could feel my hackles rising. This was starting to feel like an interrogation.

'It's my Russian wages.'

She arched her eyebrows even further.

'I hope you haven't been printing these or anything,' she smiled, half-joking, but actually, not really joking.

I smiled back, 'No, because that would be illegal.'

Honestly. Banks spend all their time persuading you to deposit money with them, and then when you oblige with a whole lot, they start accusing you of being a criminal. As if *they* can talk, when you consider the dodgy practices that banks have been involved in over the last few years. I wondered where this was heading. Was she about to call the police?

'Oh, and I've also got this,' I said, fishing out a purple five hundred euro note, which had been festering in my wallet for ages – the remnants of a previous work trip to Spain where I had been told to stay in a hotel for several nights, but had ended up being summoned back early, and completely forgotten about the unused hotel money. 'Perhaps you could change it into sterling for me?'

By this time, two of her colleagues behind her had stopped what they were doing (which wasn't a lot from what I could see) and were eyeballing me too.

'I'm afraid we don't accept those sir, due to money laundering regulations,' she said flatly.

'What? But it's legal tender isn't it?'

'I'm afraid we don't accept those, sir.'

By now, I was fuming.

'If money launderers can't use five hundred euro notes, they'll just use two hundred euro notes, and if they can't use those, they'll just use one hundred euro notes, and if they can't use those, they'll just use fifty euro notes... *Why don't we just ban money altogether and be done with it?*'

'I'm afraid we don't accept those, sir.'

By now, the whole bank was at a standstill, customers and staff, watching the altercation. I sighed.

'All right, give it back, but put my money in please, preferably without the interrogation. This isn't Guantanamo Bay.'

She did so, in silence. What a palaver. However, at least I didn't get a knock on the door from the police. But try it

213

yourself for a laugh – mention in passing to a bank clerk as you hand over some money that you've just come back from a trip to Russia and that you found the money in a black suitcase near the Kremlin and watch as they hit the red alert button under the desk.

With more time on my hands, I then travelled to the nearby town of Reading, the centre of which had a rather good retail complex. Quite unexpectedly, I met a guy whom I used to work with many years ago. A short, blond-haired, and in my opinion, somewhat smarmy type, yet he did seem to attract girls in worrying abundance. I think it was because of the rather impressive (albeit second-hand) sports car he used to arrive to work in, dressed gratuitously in full *Top Gear* Stig-style racing suit. Girls do seem to go for guys with fast cars; maybe they think it's rogue-like and exciting, or something. Either way, it worked for him. Scumbag.

Anyway, there he was in the centre of town with his microphone and recorder (show-off car parked up on the kerb) asking members of the public questions about God knows what for a political radio programme. And he still had that annoying smirk on his face and vaguely patronising stare.

'So, what are you doing these days?' he asked.

'I work for Russia Today TV,' I replied.

'Oh my God, isn't that the mafia state TV station funded by the Kremlin? Don't they tell you what to say?' he scoffed.

Here then was the very reason for the existence of the RT news channel. For Russians, it was to act as a balance to this kind of self-important glib statement from someone who probably knew little about the country, let alone its TV stations. My Russian colleagues at RT would often ask me the following question: 'What is the BBC other than a state-funded broadcaster?' They would tell me to consider every Royal Wedding and every Royal Baby story that the Beeb has ever covered. 'It's basically wall-to-wall positive coverage of the ruling British elite, right? No dissent allowed. Yet if a speech by a member of the ruling Russian elite is given continuous airing on RT, everyone says, "Oh look, they're just doing what they're told."' Did the Russians have a point? Well, whether you regard it as a political mouthpiece or a cultural counterbalance, let's be honest, it's not the only one. The France 24 television station, Germany's Deutsche Welle, Turkey's TRT channel... all giving their (impartial or biased?) views on the world. Back to Reading...

'So, how's your report going then?' I asked.

'Well, I've spoken to a few punters, but none of them are really saying what we want.'

'Oh, I see, so someone on high has told you what they want the punters to say, eh?'

Pause, while he digested my point.

'Ah, yeah, right, but it's not the same is it...?'

I sighed to myself. Still, he was actually a decent guy and I was probably still smarting (after all these years?) over his success in chasing a particularly attractive lady whom I had been sorely attracted to myself. What on earth had she seen in him? (His car Cary, his car.) Anyway, I left him to smarm over some more unsuspecting members of the public before contemplating more of Britain's contrasts. The trees and fields were greener than I remembered – somehow all the foliage in Russia had a greyish tint to it, probably through years of sprouting up through choking pollution. Also, people in the UK said, 'Thank you' when you opened the door for them, or, 'There you go' as they gave you change in the supermarket. Or 'Hiya' as they greeted you. It's these small things that you notice, as for several months now they'd been conspicuously missing from my daily routine. I stayed just a few days more to see friends and the like before boarding an Aeroflot flight back to Moscow. This time, the Russian men behaved themselves on the plane, and I had no complaints.

So that was my first trip away, touching base in the UK to see how I felt about it now. Anyone who has ever lived in a foreign country comes out of the experience as a changed person. They might not even know it, or even realise it's happening, but it is, and when you go back from whence you came, you often find yourself like a fish out of water; somehow not quite in sync with what everyone is talking about, or what everyone finds so important. After a length of time in Russia, I was not remotely interested in who had won *The X Factor* or *The Apprentice*, or how many bins you now had to separate your recycling into, or which footballer had been flirting with which WAG. All these things now seemed remote and unimportant, yet everyone in the UK seemed to be endlessly banging on and on about this kind of stuff. In Russia, tittle-tattle does not matter. Survival does.

Quick history lesson. Ukraine lies to the south-west of Russia and was once in the Soviet Union (part of it would later be controversially annexed by Russia). Since its breakaway back in 1991, there had been tension within the country between those who worked in big industrial towns and saw themselves aligned with neighbouring Russia to the east, and those who lived in the more cosmopolitan areas including the capital Kiev and wanted to embrace European-style capitalism to the west. The first hurdle I had to negotiate before going to Kiev was buying a train ticket. A word of advice. At train stations in Russia, the best thing to do is throw away your pocket dictionaries and just speak English. I know that sounds defeatist, if not colonialist, but actually it's just practical. Life in Russia is usually the opposite of what you know and understand to be culturally correct. In Moscow, if you try to speak Russian and don't get it exactly right, you will be summarily dismissed as a stupid foreigner. Yet, if you speak English loudly and confidently, you will receive a smile and an, 'Oh, you're from London!' and they will be more helpful. I promise you, this strategy worked hundreds of times. It's because an English-speaking person still evokes a feeling of something glamorous and other-worldly to Russians, especially if you are a Brit. Sherlock Holmes, Shakespeare, Winston Churchill... they all remind Russians of what they viewed as an unreachable world of civility and sophistication, in stark contrast to the harsh ugliness of life in the Soviet Union; whereas a person who can't speak Russian, is just a person who can't speak Russian. So my, 'Do you speak English?' strategy was not at all a reflection of ignorance on my part. In every other country I have ever travelled to, I have always tried to speak some of the local lingo, but in Russia, it just didn't seem to work. So, back to the train station...

'Do you speak English?'

She smiled.

'A little. I get Sergey, he speak bit English.'

Sergey duly popped out from around the back and processed my ticket without any of the usual fuss, hassle or snarling. Job done. A return train ticket to Kiev. At this point, I must beg for forgiveness from Ukrainians everywhere, because to me the journey turned out to be far more interesting than Kiev itself. It was to be an overnight train, taking around ten hours or so and what a delight it was. Not because it was luxurious and modern – quite the opposite. Imagine a U.S. Cold War propaganda film, featuring an old steam-powered train with those wonderful corridors and private compartments and the reassuring 'da-dum-da-dum, da-dum-da-dum' of the train's wheels clattering along the track, with compartment window frames made out of wood, and the ticket inspector knocking on the door and saying, 'Tickets please' in a clipped Eastern European accent or other. Well, that's exactly what it was like. Only then did I begin to comprehend just how vast Russia is, with its seemingly endless miles of flat, grey-green scenery, interspersed by the occasional forest, as the train intersected tiny villages – sometimes with a few inhabitants just standing and staring as we sped by. But soon the sun went down, leaving me to experience what felt like a real leap into the unknown, scary yet exciting. Just blackness outside the window, hours and hours of blackness, with only the clatter of wheels for company. It was eerie and frightening, as if Mother Russia was revealing her true nature, and could at any time cloak me in darkness and snuff me out.

I looked around at the bare but functional train compartment. A long piece of sponge on a bench for a bed, a fold-down table and a tiny TV up in the corner, showing a patriotic Soviet war film. The compartment was no more than five feet wide, with a window on the far side to observe the passing blackness. Soon I had fallen asleep on the sponge, but woke up in the middle of the night when I sensed the train had stopped moving. I looked out of the window. Darkness and silence. So weird not to hear the rumble and whoosh of traffic, or any other trappings of city life. Just a deep nothingness. We had arrived at a platform in a one-horse town in the middle of nowhere. From the far side of the platform there was only dark forest for what I imagined would be miles on end. I could now hear voices and footsteps approaching from down the corridor of the train, and soon there was a stern Russian voice and a tap at the sliding door. All bleary-eyed I opened it to find a uniformed guard, with an oversized peaked cap, who had got on the train for the sole purpose of checking passports. A young chap with dark hair and keen eyes, he scrutinised my passport with incredulity. It was as if he couldn't understand why a foreigner would be on this train in the first place. He flicked the pages, then looked at me, then flicked them again.

'You live Moscow?' he asked.

'Yes, I'm just going on a trip to Kiev.'

More flicking through my passport before disappearing down the corridor with my document, whilst offering no explanation. How very Russian. I wondered if I would even get it back. I looked out of the window at the empty grey platform, now illuminated by two neon lights which had begrudgingly flickered into life. The young security guy eventually returned and handed me back my passport, much to my relief. Now fully awake, I wandered down the train corridor to the cafeteria area. It was full of all sorts. Young couples, old ladies and groups of men drinking copious amounts of vodka. One of the guys spotted me and beckoned me over to his table where he was chatting boisterously to his three mates. He was a large, jolly fellow with a blond mop of hair; he reminded me of the former Mayor of London (later to be UK Foreign Secretary) Boris Johnson, though instead of a posh comedy voice, he was reeling off (and reeling around while doing so) a stream of incomprehensible Russian, and a tiny bit of English.

'Drink, drink! Is good, yes?'

'Yes, great thanks,' I responded, as the four of them took turns to slap me vigorously on the back, almost causing me to regurgitate the shots of vodka they had poured me. For a good hour it was vodka and gherkins all round, while in between the smiles and drinking, he insisted on pulling my face to his chest while exclaiming something loud and self-evident, to the nods and affirmations of his mates. I soon got the idea that this was all part of the social scene of travelling on trains in Russia, far removed from the 'don't talk to me, I am reading my book' atmosphere you get on British trains. Here, you must join in and celebrate a journey away from your cares, a journey which usually took hours and hours, a journey where you had an excuse to meet and greet other people in a way which never happened in the streets of Moscow. Russians have no problem travelling twelve hours overnight on a train just to visit someone for a day, and then return soon after. For us, a long journey seems a waste of time, but for them it's all part of the visit itself; a release and escape from the daily hurdles of life in a former communist state.

Suitably sozzled, I went back to my carriage for another snooze and before I knew it, the train had arrived at Kiev's main train station. Jumping off the carriages, the throng of new arrivals struggled along the platform with an unfeasible number of bulging suitcases and packages. There was an unofficial postal system in place on all trains in Russia. Basically, if you had a big package to deliver to someone in a far-flung region, sending it by post was too expensive, too slow, and was likely to never arrive. So instead, you would pay a total stranger a few roubles to take a package for you, if they happened to be travelling to the destination of your choice. If the package was particularly large, then for a few roubles more the train guard would find a space for it somewhere and watch it for you. Amazingly, this off the radar system worked brilliantly. Little ever got stolen, because if it did, then the system would break down, and that wouldn't be to anyone's advantage. To me, this unwritten world was truly fascinating. An elegant, people-inspired solution to an everyday problem, something that could not happen back home. I mean, would *you* agree to carry a strange package on a train from someone who suddenly accosted you on the platform? No, me neither.

As I negotiated the sea of arrivals with all their bags and 'post', I could hear a triumphant fanfare of some sturdy marching Soviet-like composition or other being blasted out by every ancient speaker on the platform. In the past, it would have been a reminder to you of how great it was that those in charge had succeeded in taking you from one place to another and had actually allowed you to do it, and as such, you should be grateful. Now though, it sounded rather daft. And that is where my trip essentially started and ended all at the same time. As I said, Kiev was architecturally impressive, but not different enough from where I had been living to make me feel astonished. It was like a slightly more sophisticated Moscow; a prettier city with a less macho atmosphere, but that was about it. After all, it used to be part of the Soviet Union, so you'd expect much of that era to have survived both physically and socially. As I say to all Ukrainians, please don't hate me. I'm sure there's much more to your city than I managed to observe on my own, and maybe I'll return one day to do it justice. As I had been reliably informed, Ukrainian women were indeed attractive, though on this occasion I didn't manage to make a 'connection' with anyone. And in any case, the female population were certainly not there for my benefit – Casanova, I am not. So, I walked around and saw the sights, then took the train back. That's just how it goes sometimes.

My next trip was to Latvia, a small Baltic state to the west of Russia that had declared independence from the Soviet Union in 1991 and later joined the European Union. I thought it might be a good idea to visit a former Soviet country, where around a quarter of the population were ethnically Russian. I went with my aforementioned bohemian Irish friend Conor. We had heard that the capital Riga was the place to go – historic, charming and laid-back. It turned out to be the complete opposite. But first, when we arrived at the departures area of Moscow's Sheremetyevo airport, I looked up at the board, but could not see our flight to Riga.

'Conor, our flight's not there,' I said, pointing.

'What?'

He took out the booking form and examined it. Suddenly, an exclamation from Conor, as his face went white.

'Feck!'

All the details were fine, except… we had somehow contrived to arrive at the wrong bloody airport. Conor (not the most organised person in the world, bless him) had booked everything, but forgotten to check the printout, and there was no time for us to make it to the correct airport, which was on the other side of the city.

'Conor, I'm going to kill you.'

We quickly discussed our options and instead of allowing me to end his life, we decided to fork out for an expensive slightly later flight. The logical thing would have been to abandon ship, return home, and use the money for a night out in Moscow. But mentally we were both prepared for an exciting trip away, and it's difficult to put that optimism back in its box. We should have known better. A bad omen is a bad omen.

When we finally arrived late at night in Riga, we took a small airport bus to the centre of town, as we had overheard a Latvian lady telling a tourist how half the local airport taxis were part of an organised tourist rip-off scam. Fifteen minutes later we alighted in town, but almost the moment we set foot on the cobbled stones of the old quarter, a local man who was getting out of a nearby taxi regarded us with unprovoked hostility.

'Motherfuckers! Arseholes!' he glowered.

What a welcome. Ignoring him, we trudged on looking for our hotel, passing side streets full of drunk youths and young weary-looking police. Pretty soon, we realised what the scene was here. Basically, the Latvians disliked the Russians, the Russians disliked the Latvians, and everyone disliked the drunk stag party Brits who staggered around town chanting English football songs while urinating on Latvian monuments. It was a horrible brew. And then there were the local women, some of whom seemed blatantly geared up to fleece you as a foreigner. We made the monumental mistake of chatting to a couple of girls in a bar who accepted our offer to buy them some drinks. The mistake was, we let them choose the drinks. Then the bill arrived. Our jaws dropped. It was the equivalent of two hundred dollars, for four drinks. It turned out that they were in cahoots with the bar owners to bleed stupid foreigners dry and get a cut of the ill-gotten proceeds. We paid the money and left the bar with our tails between our legs. From that moment on, I was wary of talking to anyone at all. We had been verbally abused and financially screwed within two hours of arriving. And then there was the door policy of bars and clubs. With all the rowdy stag parties going on, many places had decided to arbitrarily ban all foreigners. You'd go up to the entrance of a club, where clearly there were hundreds of people within, and the bouncer would look you in the eye and say, 'Sorry, it's a private party' or, 'Sorry, you have to pay two hundred dollars to reserve a table before you can come in.' This kind of attitude is where I draw the line. In 1960s Britain, Irish and Caribbean migrants who were looking for somewhere to rent would be confronted with signs outside houses saying, 'No Irish, no blacks, no dogs.' It's no way to deal with a situation. You ban people because they are rowdy or drunk, but not because of their ethnicity, otherwise you end up with something called fascism. It's obvious, isn't it? Well, clearly not in this former Soviet state. And indeed, there had been a few Nazi-style marches in Riga, made up of Nazi-sympathising knuckleheads. In all, as you can tell, I didn't like it. Except for the small museum of Latvian photography – an unassuming building down a tiny cobbled side street, containing the oddest photographic artefacts and some very old haunting photos of people from Latvia's history. As ever, no one ever seemed to smile in photos in those days, did they? From peasant farmers to land-owning aristocrats; always deadly serious as they stared unblinking into the camera. So all in all, what did I make of Riga? Well, from what little I saw, let's just say it wasn't for me.

Having abandoned Latvia (well in fairness, just the country's capital) the next destination on my whistle-stop month of travel was to be Saint Petersburg, Russia's second largest city situated to the north of Moscow. I took a new high-speed train there; this was no old-style clackety-clack train, but a full-on modern bullet-type thing, with comfy seats, soundproof windows and reassuring announcements in different languages. It turned out, however, that the windows were not just thick in order to keep out the engine and wheel noise. The expanded train line had been built at the expense of many communities along the route, which had either been cut in half, or had had their local train services wiped off the map in order to accommodate the new super-fast gleaming piece of transport engineering. As a result, many bitter residents would lie in wait for the zooming train to go by, before launching a hail of stones at the carriages. By the time we got to Saint Petersburg, the train had sustained not inconsiderable damage – I counted three half-smashed windows and two severely dented doors. They must have kept a whole load of spare parts at both destinations for this eventuality. I checked into my hotel and quickly went out to explore. People rave about Saint Petersburg. They say it's cultural, enigmatic, beautiful and lots of other complimentary stuff. Well, sorry, but I disagree. The thing is, there are two types of city break travellers. Those who want to endlessly visit churches and museums, and those who don't. I am in the latter group, which makes it difficult to actually find anything else to do in Saint Petersburg, as the place is *full* of churches and museums.

When you've seen one ornate church, you've seen them all as far as I'm concerned. Once inside, I can't help thinking that the humble carpenter of biblical times would have been appalled to see his likeness on the cross hanging up between all the gold, priceless frescos and other valuable stuff, which no doubt he would suggest should be sold off and the money given away to the poor. And then there are the museums – why do they always have to be so dull? It's as if the curators are making every effort to make the art as non-interactive as possible. Paintings hanging neatly on white walls, all pristinely and clinically labelled and dated, with security guards watching your every move, waiting to pounce if you have the audacity to touch anything, while tourists tramp around staring at everything as if they have any clue at all what each piece of art is all about. Even worse, are the guided city tours. At one point, I was walking over a bridge (there are many wide waterways in Saint Petersburg) and came across a gaggle of visitors being told all about some ancient marketplace or other.

'And this is where the merchants would buy and sell their goods at the marketplace,' explained the guide to a group of attentive Finnish tourists. 'They would pull up their horse-drawn carts here before offloading the food they had gathered from the countryside and woven fabrics they had made themselves.'

Well, there's a surprise. Imagine if in two thousand years' time some guide was showing people how we shop today.

'And here is where people used to wheel around metal

things called shopping trolleys, before using an ancient form of currency called money.'

I mean, who cares? They were all just people like you and me, trying to earn a living, or just doing the weekly shopping. Why tourists find this sort of thing interesting is a mystery to me. The truth is, what makes or breaks a city is the nature of its people in the present, not the past. Are they welcoming and friendly, or aggressive and unkind? Surely, a city should not be measured by how many Picassos or Renoirs it has hanging on the walls of its museums, or how many churches it can boast, but by its atmosphere, food and vibrancy. I mean, look at Paris – just because it houses an overrated painting of a woman who can't smile properly, does not in itself make it a 'must see' destination. For me then, I reckoned Saint Petersburg was mediocre at best. It was also trying very hard to be 'Western'. So parts of it resembled Venice, except it's not. While other parts resembled London, except it's not. It's like a giant facade of a pretend Western city, and what's the point of that? It simply serves to take away any vestige of 'Russian-ness'. After all, if I wanted to experience Venice, I'd go to Venice. If I wanted a London experience, I'd go to London. And yet here they were, the Finnish tourists all nodding sagely at the guide, while taking photos of nothing in particular. And that, I'm afraid, was Saint Petersburg. Convention be damned, and call me a miserable old goat if you want, I just didn't like it there either.

Finally, I travelled to a large town to the south of Russia called Rostov-on-Don and what a delight it was! I stayed in a hotel right by the side of the River Don, and the weather was sunny and bright, the same way I would describe the people there. Here, the environment was better, the trees were greener, the flowers more flowery, and the people... well... just *nicer* than in Moscow. I went for a walk and immediately spotted that this town was a favourite place for Russians to tie the knot. There were weddings and wedding parties everywhere. Cars all adorned with flowers, horns beeping, with unconnected onlookers apparently allowed to join in the party with gusto. It was also a town known for its weekend street market, which was a sight to behold. Thousands of people, hundreds of stalls, with all manner of fresh food and spices on display. The region was also famous for its fish, and with good reason. I saw shoals of still-alive fish, flapping and splashing away in great vats of water, drenching nearby shoppers who just seemed to laugh it off as part of the market experience. They seemed very keen on colourful carp as a local delicacy, though we in the West are more used to keeping them as pets (if you happen to have a big pond in your garden, that is). In the evening I ventured out of the hotel and discovered a small restaurant nearby. Old and twee, like something from the 1950s, it was full of outdated Russian furniture and useless ceramic knick-knacks arranged all over the place. In the main room there were several small tables and one long table running from one side of the room to the other, which was being used by what was probably a wedding party. Boisterous and on the edge of serious drunkenness, the group of party-goers, uncles, aunts, cousins and hangers-on all suddenly stopped talking and regarded the interloper as I ventured inside. Silence befell the entire room, while they stared at me as if it was the strangest thing they had ever seen – a tourist in a traditional restaurant, and an Afro-Caribbean one at that. It was as if my arrival had suddenly sobered them all up. Then abruptly the silence was broken by what could have been the groom, who stood up, drink in hand, swaying slightly. A huge smile suddenly broke out on his face, as he raised his glass.

'Obama! Obama! Obama!' he yelled with glee. The chant was taken up by all the others in the party.

'Obama! Obama! Obama!' they all screamed in welcome, with smiles on their faces, while starting to clap in unison. If there's one thing Russians know how to do, it's how to clap in time. It must have been all those years of being forced to listen to clipped Soviet marching music. I decided to take their unconventional welcome in the spirit that it was meant. If the same thing had happened in a bar in America, I would probably be filing a lawsuit for racial stereotyping. But out here in the wilds of Russia, none of these folk had probably even seen a black guy in real life, let alone in their local eatery. They had somehow managed to be racist and friendly all at the same time; no mean feat. I revelled in my new-found fame and also in some tasty local fish and the inevitable rounds of vodka. Rostov-on-Don, the true spirit of Russia and the Russians I decided.

After a few more very pleasant days there, it was time to leave the banks of the River Don and return to Moscow, with my spirits raised. Though before I got there, the plane journey back was to be a test of that spirit. The most turbulent flight I have ever taken in my entire life. For the first forty minutes or so, nothing out of the ordinary happened, just the usual two annoying people next to you who won't stop talking loudly to each other, the annoying queue at the toilets which magically appears the moment you get up to go yourself, the annoying announcements made by the captain which wake you up just as you've drifted off for a snooze. And outside the window all seemed fine, with clear skies, sunshine and nothing to trouble us. Yet without warning, the plane suddenly lurched to one side as it began to be buffeted by the most tremendous winds. As a frequent flyer I largely ignored it to begin with, pitying the panicking passengers around me as they gasped in terror. But when I saw the look of horror on the flight attendant's face and the way she ran to the back of the plane to grab the intercom, I knew that this was to be no ordinary buffeting.

'Vsem ostavat'sya na mestach i pristegnut'remni!' she yelled. ('Sit down and put your seats belts on!').

I had never heard a flight attendant shout so loudly. The plane was dipping and diving probably hundreds of feet at a time, the wings were bending to the point where I thought they were going to snap in half, and the passengers were screaming their heads off. For once, the drunk Russians in the aisles were puking up due to something other than inebriation. Me, I was gripping the hand rests with genuine fear. The wide-eyed looks I exchanged with the two previously yacking middle-aged Russian women sitting to my right said it all. Up to that point in the flight we had largely ignored each other, but now we were eyeballing each other like we were the last humans we would ever see in this life. On and on it went, while I wondered what would happen if the plane actually flipped over. Would that still be a recoverable situation? I made a mental note to ask a pilot that question, if I actually got out of this alive. And then suddenly... it was over. The plane just stopped listing, though everyone was silent, fearing that perhaps we were just in the eye of the storm. Plastic food containers were strewn all over the place, with coffee and tea splashed on the seats and people's clothes. No sound, except the whirring hum of the engine, and the rattle of a child's toy as it rolled down the aisle before coming to a stop against the wheel of an upturned food trolley. Then, the captain's slow voice, with classic Russian understatement, crackled into the silence.

'We have now passed through the area of turbulence.'

Area of turbulence. No kidding. I looked at the women to my right. They were still aghast with disbelief. I looked down at my still tightly clenched fists, finally letting go of the hand rests to reveal my sweating palms. Fuck me, that was no joke. As the flight returned to something like normality, the two Russian women bought themselves some vodka and spontaneously bought one for me too. I accepted, and we raised a glass (well, plastic cup) to survival.

And so ended my month outside of Moscow. On my return to the airport I took the new Aeroexpress train back to the centre of the capital. A clean, fast, glitzy, punctual service which cost the equivalent of six pounds for a one-way ticket. And no terrifying turbulence. Superb. The only bizarre thing was the announcement over the speakers as we were about to pull away from the platform.

'It is strictly forbidden to transport explosives or chemicals on this train.'

Explosives or chemicals. Hilarious. Imagine the scenario:

'What's that you have in your rucksack, sir?'

'A chicken wrap and a bottle of water.'

'Are you sure? It looks like dynamite and a flask of sulphuric acid to me. I will have to ask you to leave the train...'

As we sped back towards the city, with the outlying scrubland rapidly turning into denser suburbs before giving way to concrete blocks, I have to say I was excited to get back to the capital. So far, it had been more outlandish than I could have imagined. And still I wanted more, including the elephant-in-the-room issue, which had been bugging me more than anything else. In a city of quite patently available, intelligent and charming women, I still hadn't found my soulmate. What was holding me back? In my heart of hearts I knew the answer, but was I prepared to confront the internal moral conflict which I had so effectively managed to suppress thus far?

It was time to face the music. Or at least that had been the plan, until...

10

FRACTURES

'The ground was shaking and the noise was phenomenal'

Coming back to Moscow was just as big a revelation as being away for a month had been. For one thing, summer had already given way to winter. But more importantly, my time in the UK in particular had uncovered how far my attitudes to life had been altered due to my time in Russia, and not all of it was good. In Moscow, where 'men are men, and women are women' I was finding that instead of analysing these strange social norms with detached interest, like some kind of anthropological researcher, I was actually becoming somewhat part of it. There was once a programme on the BBC where the celebrated naturalist David Attenborough famously attempted to film a group of mountain gorillas. He approached them by acting like they did, making the same noises, using the same mannerisms, essentially pretending to be an ape, until finally it happened – the gorilla group accepted him as one of theirs, albeit temporarily, allowing him to loll around with them, and in the process producing one of most amazing pieces of natural history ever broadcast on British television. This was no easy or safe task, as one wrong move and any male gorilla could have ripped his arm off with ease, or simply battered him to death. Taken to the extreme, and if Attenborough had continued to 'live' within the gorilla family, how long would it have been before he started questioning himself, wondering if to some extent, he *was* a gorilla? Actors often spend weeks on end getting into character for a specific role, a vicious gangster, for example, until they feel they *are* that gangster. But once their role has ended, how much of the character they were playing still remains within the real person? Surely, something has been unleashed which cannot always be easily put back into its psychological box, and you need another acting role for this new-found energy to be released; it can become an addiction. And for sure, cavorting with Moscow women was what I imagined getting hooked on drugs would be like. It seems fabulous at the time, but then reality hits home and you need another fix to bring you back to the initial high, whilst gradually your physical and mental health deteriorates. The problem was that each time, I needed a bigger fix, which inevitably cost more money (how many more expensive restaurants could I realistically afford?). I was in real danger of being left penniless, and with nothing worthwhile or long-lasting to show for it. One rainy Saturday, I was walking through one of the many underpasses that allow you to cross underneath the wide car-clogged roads. As I got to the far exit it started to rain quite heavily. I stopped for a moment and pulled out the umbrella I had with me. Many other people were doing the same thing, except a tall, athletic girl who, despite the chilly weather, was wearing no more than tennis shorts, a thin top and a cardigan. She was just standing there next to me, languid arms to her side, a long-strapped handbag dangling from her fingers. Clearly, she didn't have an umbrella and was looking up at the sky, wondering how to avoid getting her brunette locks soaked in the rain. I went up to her.

'Would you like to share my umbrella?'

She looked at me somewhat suspiciously, but nodded her head, and off we went. A gorgeous stranger who I had literally just met, with her hand now encircling my arm, walking down the street with me. What a buzz. What a high. My heart was singing in the rain. The sort of thing that can only happen in Moscow.

'Where are you going?' I enquired.

'I need cash machine,' she shrugged, her long brown hair swishing from side to side as her catwalk legs propelled her along the pavement with exquisite precision. She could not have been much more than twenty-five years old. Suddenly, I wondered if she was going to ask me for money, and if I had just unwittingly picked up a working girl. But no, we found a cash machine and I continued to hold the umbrella over her head as she took out some notes.

'Would you like to go for a drink with me?' I asked daringly.

'Okay.'

As simple as that. I am not exaggerating how quickly this happened. Within five minutes, I was buying her (expensive) cocktails at a fancy bar, and all this during the middle of the day. Her English was limited, as was my Russian, so we communicated mostly by drawing things on bits of paper, which was fun for a while, but how long can you keep that up for? Well, just about long enough to sustain three rounds of cocktails, before exchanging email addresses and saying goodbye. This kind of thing was not a relationship that had a future, and I could tell that I was starting to have a problem. And here's what it was: an average-looking forty-something Western bloke who gets a lot of attention from stunning twenty-something Russian women tends to imagine he is more attractive than he really is. If he is going to live in Russia for the rest of his life, and fully immerse himself in the cultural norms (rightly or wrongly), then it doesn't really matter. But if, realistically, he intends to return to the West, he will then have to suddenly give up his 'drug' and go cold turkey, and as most ex-drug addicts will tell you, that process is very hard work indeed, with a real risk of psychological damage in the process. So once back in Moscow, I again found myself back on the treadmill of getting girls' phone numbers and spending lots of money taking them out to restaurants and buying them presents. I say treadmill because each failed attempt was leaving me listless and unfulfilled. I was starting to feel morally bankrupt and not at all happy. Each baffling encounter seemed to drain away a little of my soul, as I started to yearn for a woman who actually liked me for who I was and not just for how many bottles of perfume I was likely to buy her. As Winston Churchill once famously said, when referring to Russia:

'It is a riddle, wrapped in a mystery, inside an enigma.'

This also seemed to apply to its womenfolk. Added to this, I could see another potential problem. I had a friend, a Swedish guy, who was living with a Russian girl in a nice central apartment in the city. He was as happy as Larry. But every month (sometimes every *week*) she was pestering him to marry her. In her eyes, marriage meant financial stability and without it a girl had nothing. She had also come to the conclusion, quite reasonably, that if he suddenly had to return to Sweden, she would not be able to go with him if they were not married, due to visa restrictions. This was a good point and one that was not lost on my friend. However, all this began to put pressure on the relationship. He was basically faced with having to marry someone whom he was not necessarily entirely sure of as yet, while she was faced with potentially having to jump ship to find someone who *would* marry her without any prevarications. For her, time was running out. Such was the culture, that in her eyes, her looks would not last forever. All of this was straining their relationship to breaking point. The question was, did I really want that kind of pressure? After all, it seemed that every Russian woman I had met was at some point after a marriage partner, sooner rather than later. This also meant that any preconceived clichés I had garnered over the years about Russian women were turning out to be basically true – many *did* seem pretty much hooked on the idea of getting married to Western guys, and real quick. This was strangely disappointing, but the truth is the truth, and there you have it. Though I suppose you could turn this on its head and say that Western guys in Moscow had become hooked on the idea of getting married to a 'Russian bride'. After all, wasn't that my aim? Yet, was anyone likely to refer to me as a 'British groom'? Probably not.

Another unsettling reality I had discovered was that the sense of community that you and I may take for granted seemed somewhat lacking in Moscow. For example, one day there was a knock at my door. It was George, the socialite.

'Cary, there's a lady in the apartment across the way who seems to be in some distress.'

I followed him to the balcony of his apartment, and sure enough in the block opposite about thirty metres away, there was an old lady with a bloodied nose who was beckoning for help from her rear balcony, frantically bashing a metal pot against the railings in a bid to attract attention. At that distance, we could not tell what was wrong with her and our attempts to shout across in our poor Russian had not worked. Yet despite it being an eight-storey block, full of people in their apartments, no one else had come to their balcony to see what the noise was about. Just two expats with bad Russian, trying to visually work out which apartment she was in, as the maze-like nature of the complex made it difficult to be sure exactly which apartment was hers and how we would reach her, as the communal doors were always locked and needed various codes. Then above us I saw two Russian men on their balcony. They were fixing a satellite dish to the wall.

'Hi, do you speak Russian? The lady over there seems to need some help,' I said, pointing.

One of the men looked up with disinterest.

'Oh, it's okay, I saw a girl in there earlier.'

And that was it. Not, 'Let's try and help her somehow, maybe she needs an ambulance.' I was angry and disgusted. Maybe the 'girl in there' was her daughter who had collapsed with a heart attack. Maybe the old lady had fallen over and broken her nose. Maybe she was just a crazy old crone. Either way, the civilised thing to do would have been to go and check. But clearly, they had no intention of doing anything of the sort. So George and I ran outside, around the block and tried to gain entrance to what we thought was her section of the estate, but we couldn't even get in, as no one would answer the security buzzer, no matter how hard we tried. What a disgrace. The measure of a country is the sense of togetherness of its people, but in that moment I sensed that in Russia (or at least in Moscow) it was every man and woman for themselves. George and I returned to his apartment balcony and looked across to hers. She was gone. The door to the rear was still open, but the interior was dark – just some old clothes flapping in the chilly wind on an outside washing line. We never found out what had happened. Clearly this was to be my period of misplaced romanticism being brought right up to date with a Moscow-style kick to the groin. Or maybe this happens wherever you are; you begin your journey all bright-eyed and bushy-tailed, but gradually discover the underlying grime and pain that festers away unseen, far from the tourist sights and sounds. But there was worse to come.

I was walking along a typically icy street in Moscow, when up ahead I saw an old lady slip over and land in a painful heap on the edge of the pavement. An old lady in Russia was disparagingly known as a *babushka*. Basically, an old dear who has opinions about everything and isn't afraid to tell you at every opportunity. I think that's what the pop star Kate Bush was singing about in her song back in the 1980s, though on the other hand, and as much as I love her, who the heck knows what Kate Bush is singing about most of the time?

Naturally enough, I went to the old lady's aid.

'*Spasibo*,' she said as I helped her to her feet, which in Russian means, 'Thank you.'

'No problem,' I replied.

She dusted herself down, brushing bits of ice and snow off her old fur coat, none the worse for wear. A hardy people these Russians I thought, as I watched her continue on her way. I turned back round and took one slippery step forward.

Swish! Crump!

I found myself on the pavement in exactly the same spot. I let out a howl of indignation as I lay there for a moment stunned, cheek against the frozen ice. No one came to my aid. It had been my first fall since moving to Moscow. Not bad, considering the prevalence of hazardous snow and ice everywhere. And like all men who've been knocked off their perch, I thought to myself, 'Hey, I'll be fine; after all, I'm a man.' I gradually got to my feet, trying to ignore the searing pain in my ribcage, until finally sense overcame male bravado and I staggered into a medical centre. Numerous X-rays and scans revealed a raft of fractured ribs, which would only heal through rest, and an awful lot of painkillers. Thus began an enforced three-week confinement in my latest (yes, I had moved yet again, due to more noise problems) Moscow apartment. My moral hand-wringing over the attractions or otherwise of Moscow women, that I began the month hoping to resolve, would have to wait. Surely, this was going to be my darkest hour.

When you're younger, your only thought is the location of the next bar, and whether you can cover the cost of the beer. But when you're older, your only thought is the location of the next medical centre, and whether you can cover the cost of the treatment. How depressing. Plus, being sick and on your own at home is like stepping out of society and living somewhere in the land of limbo. When you are not working, you feel completely disconnected from everything, such is our overwhelming work ethic upbringing. No matter how legitimately ill you are, you still feel guilty about not showing up for work (except for people who have had consensual sex with the boss and can therefore get away with doing virtually nothing all year round – every company has one of those, don't they?). Then there's the paranoid feeling that everyone must be talking about you, quickly followed by a deep depression over the thought that perhaps you will never be well again, which then coalesces into thoughts of your own mortality and death. Time on your hands allows your mind to wander into territories normally hidden by the hustle and bustle of life's daily chores – you get dressed for work, you travel to the office, you interact with your colleagues, you buy food on the way home, you cook, you wash your clothes, you watch TV, you check your emails, you prepare for work the next day, and you go to bed. It's a routine which we often complain about ('Oh, the trains were terrible today, and they'd run out of my favourite muesli at the supermarket!') yet we value the routine more than we think. It gives us a sense of purpose, a sense of belonging, a sense of reality. But an enforced illness takes you away from that and banishes you into a world you are not familiar with – no routine, no connection to anyone, no purpose. You'd think it would be great. I mean, all that time off. Well actually no, because depending on your illness, you are probably not well enough to do all those things around the home you thought you would now have time for. With fractured ribs, say, you cannot reach up and change that light bulb that's been bugging you for weeks. You can't lift a medium-sized folder from the shelf to do that paperwork you've been meaning to sort out. You can't even change the sheets on your bed. Now imagine all of that, but also suffering the uncertainties of being sick in a strange land. It was like navigating a ship into seriously uncharted waters.

So I ended up lying in bed with nothing to do for weeks. Misery. I felt like that character in the book by Franz

Kafka called *The Metamorphosis*. It revolves around a guy who wakes up one day in bed to discover he's turned into a giant beetle and can't move, as he's stuck on his shell-like back and just festers there for weeks on end. It's supposed to be a critique of society and how we live, though actually it's mainly just a very boring and depressing book. Nonetheless, I could sympathise with the condition. It was impossible to sleep properly as any pressure on the ribs led to the most extraordinary pain, while trying to sleep upright didn't work either. I ended up in a kind of constant half-lying down, half-asleep, half-awake, state. And then there's the pain, which no amount of pills can disguise. Pain which seeps into the dark corners of the mind and roots itself there like a solid oak tree – unmoving and unflinching, sucking up your life force and making sure that you know about it. This was not good.

There were, of course, a couple of hours each day when I was vaguely alert, and I used those hours to sit and stare at the view from the window of my seventh-floor apartment. A small, nicely furnished affair, my new rented accommodation was highly modern by Moscow standards and suited me just fine. A bedroom just about big enough to fit a double bed, a kitchen with a bizarre yet fun montage of Laurel and Hardy, Charlie Chaplin and Marilyn Monroe painted on the wall, and a lounge with a square glass table, plus two small sofas wedged either side of a tiny computer desk. There was a ledge with a few potted plants and a door leading to a brick-sided balcony with a view of Moscow. There were snow-covered rooftops as far as the eye could see, ranging from an old tin-roofed

Soviet house opposite my block, to a huge new advertising facade in the middle distance, to a row of chimneys akin to London's Battersea Power Station on the edge of town – spewing out clouds of slow-moving white steam into the air as the industrial heating machines clunked away, keeping the city's wrought-iron central heating systems warm and defrosted against the cold. In fact, each apartment block also had its own independent generator in the basement which fed all the radiators in all the apartments of that block. These radiators were switched on for most of the year, twenty-four hours a day, and you couldn't regulate them as there was no thermostat in the apartments and no way of turning them off. The result was a stiflingly hot apartment where I would be walking around in my boxer shorts, while outside the sub-zero temperatures were busy freezing to death any living creature that dared to venture out for longer than ten minutes. A symbol perhaps of the city of contrasts that is Moscow.

As I looked outside, I saw a group of men clearing snow off the roof of an old building, with only one of them sporting a thin rope tied around his waist, attached to a chimney stack – his only means of survival if he should slip. As for the others, well, they were just taking their chances. I listened to the scraping of their shovels, followed by the 'Pffffff' sound of the snow hitting the ground. Huge icicles too were dislodged, shards falling with a splintering sound onto the pavement below, with another man below steering the walking public away from the danger zone. Many people died each year from being fatally spiked in the head by falling icicles. Elsewhere on my street I could see the remnants of different periods of Russia's history. Ornate houses fit for a Tsar sandwiched between ostentatious new apartments, all sitting uncomfortably alongside grey 1970s breeze blocks. Each new ruling elite constructing what was in vogue that decade, without a thought for what was there already. Indeed, whole swathes of historical buildings had already been swept away to make room for new apartment blocks, while a few small wooden homes, tucked away from the attentions of the bulldozers, somehow managed to survive, like tiny mammals cowering from the destructive force of some giant lumbering dinosaur. There were a few bare trees too, dotted in and around the houses and apartments; their brown skeletal branches weighed down by ice to the point where many branches simply broke off, falling to the earth with a sharp 'Crack!' And further down the street I saw a group of exquisitely dressed women duck into a posh hairdressers boutique for their weekly nail manicures and sessions trimming their already perfect blonde or jet black fringes. But how much looking out on to the street can one take? I was starting to feel like James Stewart in Hitchcock's *Rear Window*, a character who sits staring out of the window at his neighbours' lives, having been forced to stay put due to a broken leg.

I suddenly heard the sounds of a piano being played. A haunting classical composition which I was not familiar with, but could have been something like Shostakovich. Russians love pianos and it's not unusual for an apartment to come furnished with an old piano standing upright in the hallway or bedroom. The melody was emanating from an apartment across the hallway and drifting mist-like into mine. A genuinely emotive moment, which made me start to question what I was doing in Moscow. If you'd told me five years earlier that I would be living and working in the Russian capital, I would have laughed you out of town. Funny where life takes you. As the music continued to wash over me, I felt a sudden and tremendous pain in my left side and collapsed onto the floor.

When I came to, I realised that I had fainted. I had no idea how long I had been on the floor. Crawling along like an injured spider, I located my phone and rang a friend for help. Elizaveta (she of the pigs don't go, 'Oink, oink' debate) arrived to find me hunched in a chair, sobbing my eyes out and hardly able to move. A phone call to a local ambulance service revealed that they would charge the equivalent of more than one hundred pounds just to pick me up. So instead I rang the taxi driver Anton, who happened to be in town and not at his *dacha*. With the two of them helping me to walk by holding me up by my arms either side, they gingerly put me in the back of his car, flat-out, knees up.

'No worry,' said Anton, as we sped off to the hospital.

Every bump in the road was an ordeal, as Anton and Elizaveta chatted away in Russian in the front. What incongruous situations we find ourselves in sometimes. It turned out the smashed ribs had also damaged a main nerve, and the pain had simply blacked me out. Next thing I knew, a nurse was injecting a strong dose of painkiller straight into my butt with a disturbingly large syringe.

Surely, this is the sort of stuff they give to horses? Then, it was back to mine, where eventually Elizaveta and Anton said their goodbyes, leaving me with a bag of pills from the hospital which I arranged on my hallway shelf like a mini-laboratory, before curling up in bed. Time passed, and the day drifted by in a hazy kind of way. But then as if to emphasise my fragility, something very Soviet indeed happened right outside my apartment. It began with a low rumbling that was making the unwashed cutlery in my kitchen sink, start to rattle. Then the whole apartment too began to shake. Clutching my bad left side with my right hand, I staggered out of bed and went to the window to see what on earth was going on. An earthquake perhaps? Not quite. It turned out to be a large-scale military parade, which was taking place right through the residential streets of the city. There was to be a Red Square procession of some sort the following day, and this was the rehearsal for all the troops and hardware. You may have seen tanks and rocket launchers on the telly, but it's not until they rumble past you that you begin to comprehend the size and frightening power of these machines. Massive rockets too, and I mean *massive*, on the backs of even bigger transport carriers, all painted in dull military green, adorned with the white, blue and red of the Russian flag. Incredibly, they were just using normal back streets to make their way to Red Square, and on either side of the pavement people just stood and stared at these terrifying hunks of machinery as the expressionless soldiers on board guided the metal monsters to their destination. The parade went on for about twenty minutes. The ground was shaking and the noise was phenomenal. Absolutely bone-crunching. What it would be like to actually be on a field of battle with these things being used all around you, I could not even imagine. It was almost as if the government was saying to the people, '*This* is where your taxes go to keep you safe from the evil West. And don't you forget it.' How many human ribs had these tanks crushed in their lifetime, I wondered?

Time to hobble back to bed. I needed to get myself fit again and all my energy replenished, for what would be the final stretch of my time in Moscow, and for what turned out to be an encounter with the Big Man himself.

11

VLADIMIR
VLADIMIROVICH PUTIN

'For a heart-stopping moment, his gaze met mine'

A few weeks later, I had fully recovered. So much so that I agreed to help a friend with the delivery of a large, heavy sofa bed. The bed would be picked up from the furniture store by my ever-helpful man-of-all-trades taxi driver Anton, with a van he often used to transport materials to and from his *dacha*. We would then drive it to the address and take it up in the lift to the apartment. At least, that was the plan. What actually happened was that on arrival it wouldn't fit into the lift. Anton was fully prepared to just take it back to the store. But I was not content with this, as I had promised my friend she would get her sofa. Anton realised that the problem would therefore not go away. For ten seconds, he scratched his head. And then:

'Okay, we use stairs.'

The thought of lugging this thing up ten flights of narrow stairwells filled me with horror. But Anton hadn't even flinched, so I went with it. Now I'm not the strongest guy around, so this turned out to be as physical a challenge as I'd ever had, as we huffed and puffed with the sofa beast, struggling to manoeuvre it up and around the shabby banisters and chipped walls. Eventually, on the fifth floor, we came to a standstill, as for reasons unknown, the last five flights were even narrower than the ones that had preceded it. In short, the sofa bed was stuck. Another ten seconds of thought from Anton, and then:

'Okay, we take through window.'

'What?!' I exclaimed, still trying to recover my breath.

Anton pointed to the double windows of the communal stairwell.

'How are we going to do that?' I asked.

'We open windows, tie rope to sofa, then pull up sofa.'

And sure enough, that's exactly what he did. Back to the van to find some heavy-duty rope (Anton's van was a walking DIY shop), open the windows, find two burly guys on the street who would be willing to help (I had to slip them some roubles of course) then a heave-ho of the sofa up the outside of the block and into the windows on the tenth floor. Unbelievable. And yet... it worked. And as I stood by, grateful that I had been spared the physical exertions of the final push, I realised that right there in microcosm was the Russian psyche. It was a moment of pure revelation. It was as though the proverbial light bulb had just lit up over my head. *This was it!* I had finally, inadvertently, discovered what I had been looking for. Churchill's mystery-riddled enigma, solved in one. And here it is: as far as Russians are concerned, if there is a problem, you ignore it, and it will eventually go away. But if it won't go away (like my sofa dilemma) then you find the quickest solution, and just get on with it. No worrying what the neighbours might think, no worrying what the local council might think, no worrying about your own health and safety. Just, 'We have problem, we have solution, yes, we do it now.' That's it. No time-wasting. No hand-wringing. Now hold that thought and transfer it to the minds of the ministers inside the Kremlin, and you have Russian foreign policy in a nutshell. Problem which won't go away? – ten seconds of thought – solution – action. To its political foes in Europe: 'You insult us, yes? Okay, no problem, we turn off gas supply.' Just like that. No arguing. No negotiation. No messing about. For them, it's as obvious as 2 + 2 = 4. So whether it's Ukraine, Syria, or how to get an impossibly large sofa into a high-rise apartment block, the essence of it is the same. This would also apply of course to the man in charge of the Kremlin. The embodiment of the Russian psyche. A man more Russian than Russian. A man who was to cross my path for the briefest of moments.

When it comes to anecdotes, incidents and stories, you can't make things happen when you want them to. You can trundle along in your life for weeks on end with nothing in particular occurring and then suddenly everything happens all at the same time, right? And so it was that it was turning out to be a very uneventful period of time. The snow was snowing, work was working, and my money was doing what money always does when applied to too many misspent nights out – disappearing into a swirling black hole of cocktails, restaurant bills and taxi fares. But then when I least expected it, there came a real surprise. A moment I would never forget. In some ways, the moment that I had been waiting for, yet never believed would come even close to happening. An encounter with Vladimir Vladimirovich Putin, to give him his full name – the hard man of Russian politics himself. The man who had managed this most unmanageable of countries since the turn of the century. And yet for all that time in charge, what did anyone really know about him? Well, not a lot. He was born in Leningrad (now Saint Petersburg) apparently in humble circumstances, though no records appear to exist of any 'Putin' family members beyond one grandfather. Indeed, during my time in Russia I had not come across any other Russian with the surname Putin, and no one else I spoke to seemed to have either. As a kid, he liked Soviet spy thrillers, which probably fuelled his interest in becoming a KGB officer, which he achieved from the mid-1970s to the early 1990s. He had a wife (now divorced) and two daughters, though they are hardly ever seen. He speaks fluent German and more English than he lets on. Indeed, at a charity concert in Saint Petersburg he appeared on stage playing the piano and singing the Fats Domino song 'Blueberry Hill' in English, in front of a surprised audience which included Hollywood actors like Sharon Stone and Kevin Costner. Mr. P's rendition wouldn't have given Fats much of a run for his money, but hey it was for charity. Away from singing, he had a pet dog called Konni, a black Labrador retriever. And that's about it. But whatever his background, anyone who makes it through to becoming the leader of a country must possess cunning, intelligence, a degree of charm, more than an element of ruthlessness and a good dollop of skulduggery, and Putin is no exception. Obviously, part of his power derives from people's fear of his former (continuing?) KGB connections; a fear which is still pretty much all-pervading across Russian society. Information is power, a truism that has never been lost on the leader of the world's largest nation. It was Putin after all who had decided to create the TV station where I was now employed. A twenty-four hour English language news channel designed to rival all the other twenty-four hour English language news channels across the world, while spinning a Russian view of things. So it was no surprise that at some point our benefactor would want to come and visit the station to see what was being done with all the Kremlin's roubles. There was no official announcement that he was about to visit; just a rumour a few days before that someone 'important' was coming, with no names mentioned, just knowing looks from the newsroom journalists and wide-eyed panic from the managers. Suddenly, a whole army of cleaners had been drafted in, while new carpets were laid, shoddy areas painted and rooms de-junked and spruced up. Everything spick and span, ready for the arrival of the most important of visitors. And the security was mammoth, with teams of burly Russian guys inspecting every nook and cranny of the building. The only difference between all those intimidating *Men in Black* types you see hanging around the U.S. president and *these* guys, was that the Russians didn't wear shades. They don't *care* if you know who they are or not. Even the toilets were out of bounds and you were not allowed to leave your desk for your entire shift (there were queues a mile long down the corridors outside the toilets as the deadline neared).

As the hour approached, the tension in the newsroom rose and I could feel my heart pounding. Me, a seasoned journalist, getting nervous. I then used a technique I had been taught many years back as a way of calming yourself down in any situation where you were about to meet someone regarded as being important or famous. When you see them, just imagine what they might look like with their trousers/skirt down by their ankles sitting on a toilet. No, not in a pervy way – it's just that they don't look quite so frightening or intimidating in that position, do they? (This should work a treat should you ever have to meet President Trump, for example.) And in any case, I wasn't even scheduled to 'meet' Putin; I was just a bystander.

And then he arrived. A short kerfuffle by the newsroom entrance, a few security types whispering into their walkie-talkies, and behind them... there he was. Wearing a dark suit and tie combo, white shirt, greying hair neatly trimmed, keen blue eyes darting around. A shorter man than you would think given that his media image portrays him as some kind of superman – riding bareback on horses, swimming lakes, wrestling tigers and becoming a black belt at judo. Not that short men can't do these things of course, it's just that I expected someone taller and bigger. That's not to say that his presence is not big. Goodness me, it *filled* the room, as his aides and security men cleared a path in front, while keeping an eye on the rear. When he walks, he has that traditional Russian man's gait; slightly ungainly, slightly waddling from side to side, as though having a touch of rickets, a childhood disease caused by a lack of vitamin D and calcium, and a lack of enough sunlight which can lead to a softening of the bones, leaving you slightly 'bow-legged'. I surmised that in years gone by, many Russian men did indeed suffer from this due to a general lack of nutrition. His expression didn't give much away. There was a look, though, which suggested a yearning to have some fun. A yearning to break out of the leader's straitjacket. A yearning to be able to do something… well… ordinary. He had become known for impromptu visits to local supermarkets; simply wandering inside and asking the shop owners the price of the meat and fish on display. If he deemed the prices to be too high, he would instruct the owners to lower them immediately. It was partly to play up to the cameras of course, showing how in touch he was with the 'common man', but I sensed he also needed to do it for his own well-being. Leaders more often than not lose touch with reality, a symptom of being surrounded by 'yes' men and having everything done for you.

As Putin wandered around the newsroom being shown this and that, he paused every now and then to listen and occasionally nod, with an impassive expression. I somehow wanted him to break out into a big fat smile and start moonwalking or something, but that's not the Russian way. Laughing during official meetings or events is regarded as being something only slightly unhinged (or drunk) people do. In fact, anyone who displays a degree of overt public emotion is regarded with pity and curiosity – people simply wonder what strange affliction you have picked up that has made you act in this way. And in any case, small talk was not recognised to any degree. Russians don't need to break the ice – they're accustomed to it.

I sat at my desk as he drew near, until he was just four feet away. He had stopped and turned away to mutter something to one of the aides at his side. Then he turned back, and for a heart-stopping moment his gaze met mine, and there it was – all of Russia inside those piercing steely eyes. Years of hurt and resentment. The need for respect and revenge. The feeling of being set upon by the West (imagined or not). A fierce resolve never to be beaten. Never to be weak. Never to succumb to any bullying from anyone, no matter what the price. At this point I'd love to say for the purposes of my tale that I leapt up out of my desk, shook his hand and had a chat with him. But that wouldn't be the truth; I would not have been able to hold a conversation in Russian, and given that I was working for a Russian-funded TV station, that would have been a little embarrassing. I suspect too that his security posse would have pounced in an instant, and in any case, the fleeting meeting of eyes was enough. The look had said it all. I nodded my head to him, and he flicked his head upwards in reply, as if to say, 'Yes, I've acknowledged your existence, and that's more than enough for you.' He then went on his way, leaving a trail of bemused looks from the foreign journalists, practised detachment from the Russian ones and looks of sheer relief from the managers. Could I say it had been the day I met Putin? I don't see why not. It had been as near as dammit. That then was without doubt the political climax of my time here. Done and dusted.

So with the politics done, what about that Russian bride? Well, this British groom had made up his mind to give it one last push. I was a man on a not-so-secret mission.

12

RUSSIAN BRIDES

'Restaurants, sex and presents'

Sometimes in life, you just know when it's time to leave. And for me, that moment was fast approaching with Moscow. Too cold, too aggressive, too much pollution, and just too unforgiving for a man who longed for the creature comforts of his previous existence. And yet still I found myself huddling in my apartment, looking out at the blanket of snow which had covered the city, ready to face the underlying, festering, lurking issue which thus far had not been tackled. The unresolved conundrum. The case I had not cracked. The itch that needed scratching. I had left it a bit late, but the question was still there – was I going to find a Russian girlfriend, and would she become my Russian bride? And if so, could I face the ignorant scorn of friends and family back home? ('Got her from a catalogue, did you?') Did I even care what they thought? What seemed more important was whether I was comfortable with the relationship. And what exactly was that relationship to be? Because... dear reader... on the 7th of December, my birthday no less, I finally found myself hitched up with a Russian partner. Oh yes, indeed. But first, let me backtrack to the turbulent days leading up to that startling moment. I had decided to take much of December off by using what was left of my annual leave and other days owed to me, so that the coast was clear to give Moscow my final burst of desperate energy. This then, is what happened:

December 1st – My dalliances with Russian women had been exciting, but ultimately laced with all sorts of unexpected problems and cultural barriers. As if to confirm this, I received a flirty text from one of the TV make-up girls at work. In all honesty, I didn't think we would make a great couple. But when I declined her implied offer, saying I didn't want a relationship, she sent me a further text, which said it all.

Text received: Okay, no relationship. But restaurants, sex and presents, yes?

It was as if she was conducting a business deal. How depressing is that? I had also discovered that girls in Moscow had an alarming habit of not turning up for dates. You agree to meet, you get a text confirming she's on her way, and then... she fails to turn up. No phone call. No explanation. Just silence.

'George, why do they do that, what does it *mean*?' I once asked in despair. He explained.

'It means she has several blokes on the go and you could be third on the list, placed in order of how likely you are to be a viable long-term prospect.'

A somewhat cynical explanation perhaps, but it didn't sound appealing, and in any case, I was tired of the never-ending fruitless and expensive chase. Nevertheless, like a weary soldier trudging to the front line, I got dressed up and went back into battle by meeting the make-up girl and indeed giving her what she wanted (an expensive handbag). Result? A feeling of complete listlessness. A non-starter.

December 2nd – This time the field of conflict was in a posh restaurant situated near the top floor of a city centre skyscraper. There, I quickly spotted two girls in the lounge bar area. Both tall, blonde and attractive. Prostitutes or not? It was difficult to tell, and I had almost given up trying to work it out. Either way, one had the biggest and most eye-poppingly obvious silicone chest you've ever seen, with a fake bedside manner to match.

'Hi. I only like rich men, because poor men are dumb,' was her opening gambit. The other lady (who appeared to be... er... natural) seemed a lot nicer.

'Hello, my name is Oksana, nice to meet you.'

After two rounds of expensive cocktails it became clear that 'silicone' girl was going to stay at the bar in her continuing hunt for a passing millionaire, while 'natural' girl wanted to sit with me for a while at a table. I poured some obligatory champagne and we started chatting. She was thirty-five, divorced, a native of Moscow, blue eyes and a confident manner. When she discovered I was originally from London, she began telling me her one and only experience of Britain, in her Russian-accented broken English.

'I met English man on internet and he say he very rich and have house in London. So I get visa and go to London, but he have very small house and he not rich, so I leave him and come back to Russia. Then in Moscow I meet man from Holland and he want sleep with me, so I say, "Okay, how much money?" and he look surprise and say, "No, I want relationship." Can you believe?! I tell him he is crazy.'

At this point she laughed out loud and rolled her eyes skywards.

'Sex and no money? Maybe he live on moon,' she added.

She looked pointedly at me. There was a pause. Oh my God, she was expecting me to open my wallet right there in the bar.

At that moment, with the cocktails still awash in my head, the exhaustion of the chase wearying my bones and my morality teetering on the brink, the little devil on my left shoulder whispered in my ear, 'Go on, this is Russia! And anyway, she isn't on the game, it's just a cultural thing. Did you see a pimp? No. Exactly. It's perfectly healthy. So get on with it.' But the little angel on my other shoulder was saying, 'Don't kid yourself, this is your wake-up call to plan your exit from Moscow while you still have a moral compass. It can only end in tears, and you know it.'

I looked at her.

'I'm sorry, this isn't really my thing,' I said meekly.

'What not your thing?!' she fumed.

She swished away from the table in disgust, leaving me to ponder over my decision. There may be many men reading this who will laugh at my hesitation, but in the end if it's not your scene, then it's not your scene, and that's that. I mean, I knew one British expat living and working for a law company in Moscow, whose name I will keep to myself in order to spare his blushes and spare myself a libel suit. Now, here was a guy who was once as monogamous as they come, with a faithful girlfriend still waiting back in the UK. But after a few months here, he now thought nothing of spending a night in a Moscow strip club before going back to his apartment for even more action with his Russian mistress. One in London, one in Moscow, and hundreds in between. See what I mean?

December 3rd – I decided to try out a private yoga class that I had seen advertised on a flyer being given out at a local coffee shop. I felt I'd become especially out of shape since giving up the gym and was hoping that yoga would help to balance by mind, body and soul. And as terribly clichéd as it sounds, I had once tried yoga during my previously mentioned trip to India. The regular morning class I had attended in New Delhi was run by a tiny Indian guy who could contort his body into any number of unlikely positions. His parting present to me was his book of yoga, in which he wrote an inscription:

'No yoga, no life. Know yoga, know life.'

Clever.

I flagged down a taxi to drive me to the class, as it was a little out of the way. As we eventually left the perimeter of the city, the driver appeared to be taking me on a wild goose chase into the suburbs. I took out my smartphone and activated the map locator. At last, a piece of technology that I actually had to admit had some use in my life. The taxi man was in fact being completely honest, as the little blue locator dot was moving in the right general direction – he was just avoiding traffic. Still, no harm in checking, such was the strength of the self-defence mechanism I had built up as a result of living in Moscow; an ongoing mental construction of an emotional brick wall which I was beginning to dislike more every day. He dropped me off at a nondescript location, with residential blocks in every direction. I approached the nearest block and examined the flyer under the light of a dim bulb near the entrance; it had the name 'Anastasia' written on it and a phone number. I called the number. A female voice answered.

'Alloah.'

This needs some explanation. 'Alloah' was the standard way Russians answered the telephone. Strangely, it didn't really mean anything. To my ear it sounded like a mangled version of 'Hello', and indeed the theory of the origin of this very non-Russian word was that Russians had seen and heard Western diplomats on the phone during the 1980s and simply hijacked the word 'Hello', assuming that you *had* to say this when you answered before beginning your conversation, even though they didn't actually know what it meant. Was this true, or just folklore? No one seemed to know for sure.

'Hi, is this the place for the yoga; is that Anastasia?'

'*Da, da!*' (Yes, yes!).

The door buzzed open and I ventured inside. It was the usual dank, sorry interior, with a shuddering lift unwillingly taking me up to the fifth floor. The doors opened with a screech of metal against metal, as the ill-fitting parts (no doubt patched up over a number of years) struggled to work as a functioning unit. I was in a corridor with several different apartment doors to choose from, but only one was open, from which there was emanating a waft of incense. It had to be that one, mystic yoga and all that. And sure enough, inside was a modest apartment adorned with Indian rugs and Buddha statues, the room lit only by candles, with three middle-aged women and an elderly man already doing stretches on the floor. The instructor was there too, a quietly spoken thirty-something woman with short blonde hair, wearing an all-in-one navy blue yoga jumpsuit. She was sitting on the floor, legs akimbo, and her body bent forward with both hands grasping the heel of one of her bare feet. There was an old battered mobile phone next to her on the floor, its push-button keyboard and pointy aerial betraying its 1990s origins.

'I'm Anastasia, come in, join with us,' she smiled. 'If want, you go change in bathroom.'

I had brought with me a pair of comfy grey tracksuit bottoms, so I trotted off to the bathroom with my kitbag. A strange experience again, to be taking off my clothes in the bathroom of a complete stranger's apartment. No private yoga instructor in Russia would be able to afford to rent a studio in a gym, so they just used their own place – needs must in Moscow, everyone doing what they have to do to make a few roubles. And from the stuff in the bathroom

– children's clothes hanging up, cartoon character-shaped bath gel containers, two small toothbrushes – she clearly had a couple of kids. In fact, I could hear what sounded like a couple of young kids arguing next door somewhere. I wondered what kind of life they were living. I thought about children in the West with their PlayStations, Samsung Galaxies, branded trainers and the like, and compared it to what these youngsters would have had. Here, in the suburbs of Moscow, the list of possessions was probably more like a warm coat, some second-hand boots, a pair of gloves and a hot bowl of beetroot soup if you were lucky.

I went back into the room to find that Anastasia had made a space for me and laid down a yoga mat. I took my place and started copying the various body positions she was showing her students. As the only foreigner, I had aroused some curiosity amongst her class, though in fairness, they largely ignored me and continued to fully concentrate on their exercises. I kept up as best I could (yoga is surprisingly physical) even though I was nowhere near as supple as I needed to be, or as they were. It was fun though. Halfway through, one of her kids, no more than ten years old, burst into the room and ran up to Anastasia in tears. Through her blubbing, I could understand something on the lines of, 'My brother is bullying me!' Her mum calmed her down and told us she'd be back in a minute, as she took the sobbing child into another room and scolded the brother. Here she was, trying to make a meagre living out of a few yoga classes, and even that was being usurped by the task of single-handedly looking after two kids – there were no men's shoes on the shoe rack by the door, so clearly no guy around. Yes, I know, there are thousands of single-parent families living in Britain who also have the challenge of bringing up kids solo, but believe me, raising kids in a place like Moscow is as tough as it gets. She returned five minutes later, having engineered at least a temporary truce between the two siblings, and the class continued for an hour or so, ending with gentle meditative music and herbal tea, which she made for us all in her tiny kitchen. One by one, each guest finished their tea, paid their fee and departed, leaving just her and me in the room, sitting on a big rug on the floor.

'Where is your husband?' I asked.

'No husband, he leave me.'

'Oh, right.'

Silence.

'Well, anyway, thanks for the yoga class…'

I looked into her eyes and saw an honest woman who cared for her kids, but who was struggling financially to support them. An absent husband, a tough city and very little help from the state. Was I to be the quick fix for all her problems? Or could I have potentially found someone to date, who wasn't going to ask me for a 'present'? Well… not exactly.

'My phone, it not work,' she said, picking up her old phone. It was indeed falling apart. I looked guiltily at my fancy smartphone and made a mental note that I would buy her a new one. In fairness to her, she did not at any point ask me for money or presents. I left soon after (without a physical encounter, I might add) telling her

I would be free to meet for a coffee the next day if she wanted to? She readily agreed.

December 4th – I did indeed meet up with Anastasia, the venue being Starbucks; I always thought it somewhat incongruous to find an American coffee chain in Moscow, but business in the coffee world seemed to be booming. I gave her the present of the smartphone which I had pledged to her in my mind, and which I had bought that morning. She seemed genuinely delighted. It felt like I had paid her off in some way, as we both knew we wouldn't meet again; there just wasn't enough of a 'connection', even though we'd had a good conversation. We finished our drinks, she kissed me on the cheek, and we parted. You may at this point be thinking that my cultural exploration of Moscow at the start of my adventure had turned into a desperate account of my clumsy attempts to sleep with women. Well, in some respects that's exactly what had happened. The sure-footed traveller with a moral high ground to defend at the start of his journey, who had been seeking a meaningful relationship, seemed instead to be sliding clumsily downhill into a dubious relationship-bereft swamp of short-term meaningless encounters.

December 5th – I stayed in and felt sorry for myself.

December 6th – I stayed in and felt even more sorry for myself.

December 7th – My birthday. My miserable, girlfriend-less birthday. I had officially given up. It was not going to happen and my time in Moscow was nearly at an end. Forget it. But then, that's *exactly* the moment when you meet someone, isn't it? When you've stopped looking (and stopped looking desperate), that's when it finds you. As I sat in my apartment ruminating on my predicament, my phone bleeped the arrival of a text. I picked it up and opened the text. Oh my God. It was Girl 2 Olga from the speed dating all those months ago!

Text received: What you do tonight?

Here was the one woman I had not for some reason been minded to write to, even though we'd both 'ticked' each other. What a surprise! But would it be a pleasant one, especially after all this time?

Text sent: I am free :) Maybe meet for a drink? :)

Text received: Yes, where we meet?

Text sent: Meet you outside Smolenskaya Metro station 8pm :)

Text received: Okay.

Someone had once told me that women are fond of smiley faces on text messages, so the more the better I say. Hope she didn't think I was some kind of smiling fool. I got myself ready and went off to meet her. Now why would she be contacting me so long after the event? Well, as I've said before, Russians never waste anything. They hoard stuff like magpies, on the off chance that it might come in useful, and for girls that included guys' phone numbers. A girl never knew when she'd be bored or poor, so why throw away a potential free meal ticket? Yet even knowing that, I was still eager to meet her again. In truth, I couldn't exactly remember what she looked like, though she would have no trouble spotting me in a crowd of Russians. As with most women, she was late. This is a female prerogative, designed by women so that they don't have to loiter around on their own outside a Metro station or other public place, feeling vulnerable and alone. I actually think that's fair enough, but Russian women took this prerogative to the limit, and then beyond. I mean, fifteen minutes late… okay. But *fifty* minutes?

Text received: On Metro. Arrive soon.

She was texting me from the carriage on the Metro. How it was possible to get a phone signal so deep underground in Moscow was a mystery I never got to the bottom of. I mean, this does not work in any other underground system I have ever used anywhere else in the world, but here in Moscow? No problem. Had the authorities constructed a secret underground booster aerial? 'This is Russia, anything is possible.'

Ten minutes later (now a full hour late), she rose up the escalator, spotting me immediately.

'Okay we go,' she smiled, offering absolutely no explanation for her outrageous lateness. I didn't ask.

'Yes, we can walk to the restaurant,' I replied.

She was a taller girl than I remembered, though of course when you are speed dating, you are seated, so height is difficult to judge. She was wearing high heels tonight, but even accounting for that, she was still at least an inch taller than me. Dark-haired, round-faced and pale-skinned, she was definitely attractive, though in a more subtle way than most Russian girls I had met. She had a somewhat hooded look too, her brown eyes quite deep-set and guarded, like a hawk looking around for some prey. I was already fascinated.

I had booked a Chinese restaurant I knew, one of only a handful that existed in Moscow. The standard fare was on offer: sweetcorn and chicken soup, crispy duck, prawns and lobsters. There was a big bare tank full of water behind us, within which sat three miserable lobsters, waiting for their execution. I couldn't help wondering why they couldn't at least make the poor creatures' last few hours a bit less grim. Put some sand and shells at the bottom and some plants, say. And did they really have to tie their claws together? It all seems a bit cruel to me and tends to take the edge off my appetite. Still, I suppose I myself was contributing to their misery by eating in the restaurant in the first place. Anyway, back to Olga. We hit it off right away, seemingly interested in the same things, and unlike most Russian girls, she actually ate something. All the others I had met were so paranoid about their figures they hardly ate anything after 6pm, and before that only salad. She said she read tarot cards, which interested me too. I jokingly said she should do a 'reading' for the two of us, a suggestion she took completely seriously, saying she would do it that night to see whether we would be compatible as partners.

'You must respect cards, is no joke,' she said soberly.

This I had to see. I settled the bill at the restaurant without a quibble on her part (naturally) and we took the Metro back to hers. On the way home, she linked her arm into mine and we stopped for a brief smooch outside her block. As expected, she was living in a very modest shared apartment, with broken fixtures, old rickety furniture and a bathroom where the shower unit doubled as the water provider for the sink – you had to swing the hooked fitment over to the sink to wash your hands. A very Soviet arrangement, which most Russian apartments still had even today. Her flatmate was out.

'We put magic music on,' she said, fishing out an old Pink Floyd tape and putting it into an ancient clunky cassette machine.

'Yes, sure.'

As the drawn-out intro to the Floyd's 'Wish You Were Here' (they do like to compose very long songs, don't they?) wafted into the room, she beckoned me to sit on a floor rug with her as she began dealing out the tarot cards from a surprisingly pristine deck. She said she kept them wrapped up in a mystic cloth in order to 'respect' the cards. If you respect them, then they will respect you, or something like that. She began dealing…

From what I could see, she was laying the cards out in different sections to signify the past, the present and the future. Despite my scepticism of these things, I was alarmed to see the Devil card pop up.

'Does that mean I'm going to die tomorrow and be put into a vat of boiling oil and be tortured by demons for all eternity?' I chortled.

She looked at me with those keen eyes. She wasn't laughing.

'No, but still is not good.'

'Why?' I asked.

She looked down and scrutinised the cards, a frown growing on her face, as she explained the overall significance of the reading.

'We have relationship but is not good. We will fight and have many bad emotion.'

Fight? From where I was sitting, that seemed highly unlikely.

'Well, let's at least start with some good emotion,' I said, drawing her to me. We made love and for a while, all seemed rosy. I had found what I hoped would, given time, turn into my Russian bride, and anyone who thought I was mad could go jump into a vat of boiling oil. The next two nights Olga came and stayed at mine, and again all seemed rosy. Until that is when I came home from work the next day to discover that my spare keys had gone missing from the shelf by my front door. A bit odd for someone as organised as me, but I had no explanation for it. I wondered if the apartment had been burgled. All of a sudden, my front door opened behind me. I froze, thinking that the landlady had come round unexpectedly. It was Olga.

'Did you take my spare keys?'

'Of course,' she replied matter-of-factly.

'Why didn't you ask me first?'

'Why you think?' she countered.

I was stumped. The next day when I came home from work, Olga had strategically placed a load of her clothes in my wardrobe, and bags of toiletries in the bathroom. We had been seeing each other for less than a week.

'Oh, because I am here now, is easier I have things here.'

Then, boxes of shoes appeared and jewellery too. All of this time of course she was sleeping with me, which encouraged me in my stupid male way to just go along with it all, whisked along on a tide of sexual idiocy. By this time, she hadn't been to her apartment for a week, and my place was chock-a-block with her stuff.

'Olga, this has to stop, it's like you've already moved in, and we hardly know each other.'

'What stop? You no like me?'

'Yes, I do, but this is all too fast, it's only been seven days. This is not how we do relationships in my country.'

'Well, you are not in your country!' she shouted, before slamming the bedroom door in my face.

Again, I was stumped. Yet as taken aback as I appeared to be, I was also drawn to her. There was something refreshingly kamikaze about her actions, which I was unable to refrain from. We argued and then made up, argued then made up. Those tarot cards had been right. We were fighting. Not physically you understand, but certainly emotionally. My territory was being usurped, and my understanding of what a relationship should be was being directly challenged. After a tempestuous two and a half weeks, I could take no more. I kept getting the feeling she was not being completely straight with me about anything. The last straw was when she announced that she had 'lost' her passport and that the best way to prove her character to the authorities in order to get a new one was to get the support of someone who was 'connected' and who could vouch for her. Someone say who was working for a state-funded TV station. It would also be better if she got married to that person right away. She looked at me pointedly. I had known her for ten days.

'You are kidding, aren't you?' I said.

'Why I joke about that? You not want marry me? You not like me?'

I sighed.

'Olga... no more.'

It turned out that she had contacted me after splitting up with two previous guys, both of whom she'd met at the speed dating night. I was just number three on her list of foreign marriage fodder. Another one bites the dust.

December 15th – And then there was Natasha.

I mentioned Natasha to you at the very start of all my musings. The connection we had made at that business social soon turned into a blizzard of delightful intimacy. Candlelit baths with champagne on the side; walks in the park; cooking meals together... you get the idea.

'I'd like to be a fashion designer, and I want three sons,' she had asserted during pillow talk conversation about kids. No pressure then. Heaven forbid one of my scuba squadron should become a daughter. Well, all had been going swimmingly, until I went away for a few days on a pre-Christmas trip to see some relatives. When I returned to Moscow, she dumped me. Just like that. No real explanation other than, 'I just don't think we're suitable.' Translation: 'Having thought about it, I just don't think you are rich or macho enough for me.' Or maybe she'd met someone else who was just better in bed, who knows?

So she was off. Off to find the Wizard of Oz. Or failing that, off to find a man who would fund her fantasy world of genetically engineered baby-making. Here speaks a bitter man? Possibly. But with good reason. I was sorely disappointed. At this point, I could quote any number of philosophers or philosophies over what the moral of my encounters with Russian women had amounted to. But actually, I will settle for the following:

'You may find that having is not so pleasing a thing after all, as wanting.'

Plato? Aristotle? Freud? No. It was in fact Mr. Spock from an episode of *Star Trek*, and frankly, the way I was feeling, his Vulcan words of wisdom seemed to fit my situation exactly.

As I licked the wounds inflicted upon me by my various (and foolish) short-lived relationships, and with my time running out, how then would I sum up the Russians? Well, I recalled one person who had already encapsulated them, in just nine brutal words. To explain: an increasingly popular night out for Russians was going to a live gig. Many big-name rock stars were now discovering Russia – in many ways an untapped market and one that was very knowledgeable about world music. Earlier in the year I had been to see Jamiroquai, them of the funky songs and the bloke with his trademark big silly hat. They played in a huge venue on the edge of town called Crocus City Hall, and the place was packed to the rafters with screaming fans. The band were good and the visuals huge, all controlled from a central bank of remote-control equipment high up in the audience, manned by a couple of British engineers. When the show was over, I was interested to know what their experience of working with Russian engineers had been like. After all, the visiting crew would have needed to consult and co-operate with their Russian counterparts in order to erect the set and sort out the lights and sound. One of them gave me his knee-jerk sociological assessment of the Russian psyche.

'Russians are fucking stupid,' he said. 'But the women are fit.'

And there you have it. The Russians and all their history and culture condensed into nine arguably racist uncompromising words, by a roughneck British interloper. I had hoped for something more sophisticated, considered and intelligent, but sometimes the waffle of a broadsheet newspaper article can be swept aside by a concise and to the point headline in any one of the tabloids, so maybe he was just saying it like he saw it, right or wrong. Apparently, he had experienced a great deal of trouble trying to set up the rig with the Russian technicians, who seemed more interested in pleasing their bosses and cutting corners than they were in actually getting the show ready. This had largely served to form his views. And although his assessment was a bit harsh, I had indeed noticed that the more you try to point out an obvious mistake over something to a Russian person, the more they feel you are trying to humiliate them, and the worse the situation becomes. There was one time when my landlord brought round a flat-packed double bed frame that needed to be assembled. He was struggling with all the heavy boxes into the apartment.

'Can I give you some help?' I asked.

He paused in silence, and looked at me as if to say, 'Are you suggesting I am not a man?'

He then proceeded to open up the boxes and began putting the frame together. I couldn't help noticing that according to the instructions he was doing it the wrong way.

'Are you sure the screws go in there?' I asked.

He paused again and shot me another look that this time said, 'Are you saying I'm stupid?'

I watched in silence as he gradually realised he was wrong and slowly unscrewed everything to start again, while failing to acknowledge his mistake. Would you call that stupidity? Or just cultural pride?

So as I came to the end of my Russian odyssey, on my very last day I met a lovely British girl called Sarah in a café in town. She'd been on assignment in Moscow, just like me. In a way, she could have been just what I'd been looking for but had been too blind to see. She was intelligent, attractive and 100% unlikely to ask for handbags in exchange for anything. Maybe sometimes we all like to take a peek over the fence at what we consider to be 'exotic', only to discover that the neighbours are looking right back over the fence at us and thinking the same thing. Sometimes you need to appreciate what you've already got. We exchanged phone numbers and promised to keep in touch.

And so, what had I learned about the Russian mindset from my time in Moscow? Well, they treat their country like we would treat parents whom we don't have a very good relationship with. You should despise them, yet if anyone ever came up to you and said, 'Your parents are really horrible, aren't they?', you would find yourself immediately defending them, with a screech of, 'How dare you say that about my mum and dad!' Well, when it comes to patriotism, it's the same in Russia. Ask any Russian if they love their homeland and they will reply, 'Yes, of course.' But offer them permanent visas to work in Western Europe and they will all be on the next plane out. The country would empty overnight.

And what then had I learned about myself? Well, I was more resilient than I had realised. Or maybe we all draw on unexpected emotional and physical reserves when we need to, just to survive. My time in Moscow had certainly changed me, but not all for the good. I had developed a tough new outlook on life which was unfamiliar to me and slightly disturbing.

I hoped it would be put back into the dark recesses of my character from where it had been forced to emerge, once I had left Russia. It had certainly been a roller coaster experience. Fun, scary, exhilarating and potentially dangerous. I had laughed and I had puked, I had loved it and I had hated it. I had been simultaneously attracted to and repelled by the madness of Moscow. Did I want another ride? At that moment, no. Once around the deadly fairground dipper should be enough. Yet, we always recover and wonder if we should try it again. I remembered how, a few months earlier, I had returned to Gorky Park for a visit, as I'd heard it had been refurbished. Sure enough, the horrible weed-infested grounds I had once witnessed had been replaced with healthy-looking fresh green turf. There were new trees and flowerbeds, European-style cafés and bars, bandstands, a visitors' centre, dancing fountains and smiling people. Happy-looking workers were mowing and tending and serving drinks. Kids were playing in sandpits and chasing each other in delight around a huge newly created magical fairy tale crooked wooden house. Adults were conversing or jogging, and mallard ducks were waddling around quacking. This is how the whole of Russia could be if it wanted to. But here's the paradox. Russians want to be Russian, but they are also drawn to the ideals and material luxuries of the West. Right now, they don't really know how to combine the two. It's a conundrum which might tear them apart, or lead them to another path, all of their own making. For me, Russia had revealed itself to be a top-of-the-range flashy white Mercedes, with alloy wheels, leather seats and all the gadgets you could want inside. But someone had taken out the powerful engine and replaced it with something that could only run a lawnmower. From the outside it looked great, but start it up and it really isn't moving forward very fast. I had also learned that Russians don't like confrontation. If they feel threatened, they will fight to the death. But if they can avoid a confrontation, they will do so. I had often wondered why Russian bosses rarely replied to emails. My friend and colleague Peter once explained it to me.

'A Russian boss sees it like this… if you ignore an issue, it will eventually go away. But if you confront an issue, it becomes a problem.'

In the past, it was the denial of problems that had led to the downfall of the Soviet Union. So much stuff was being ignored that eventually the whole creaking system suddenly exploded into a fireball of unresolved issues.

Something doesn't work? Ignore it. The workers are upset about low pay? Ignore it. There's no equipment to fix the electricity generators? Ignore it. In the end though, there was no more room under the carpet to sweep everything, and 'BANG!'; it all blew up in their stoical blank faces. From what I had seen, there was a real danger the same thing could happen to Russia. To me, it seemed like a slightly smaller version of the Soviet Union, with a veneer of modernity, which so far had not taken root in anything other than bells and whistles.

And what of the Russian people? It was my hope they would drag themselves out of the morass of the past and look towards the future, though I suspected it would take another social, even revolutionary, upheaval to do so. This would not necessarily involve violence, and not even 'revolution' as we understand it. I didn't want to stick around to witness it though; I was no rabble-rouser and my own emotional upheaval had been more than enough, thank you.

I had already packed most of my bags and said my goodbyes to the friends I had met along the way. I wouldn't be staying for the New Year firework celebrations in Red Square – surviving this strange culture was celebration enough for me, and I had always hated holding leaving parties (you always get a few people turning up who you don't like, or hardly anyone turning up at all, meaning they don't like *you*). For me, it's more dignified to just slip away quietly.

On the final walk back to my apartment, I witnessed a traffic jam, with an ambulance, blue lights flashing and sirens blazing, stuck behind three lanes of stationary cars. And yet no driver was making any attempt whatsoever to move aside and let it through. Suddenly, I stumbled over something hidden in the deep snow, what I initially thought was a tree root growing up through the pavement. I looked back to see what it was and noticed something protruding. I peered closer. It was a hand. I gingerly moved away some of the snow around it to reveal an arm. The hairs on my neck pricked up. It was my second dead body. Sometimes, men here would get so drunk that they would pass out on their way back from the bar, leaving the thickly falling snow to cover them up without a trace. They would simply suffocate or freeze to death, unlike the vodka in their now rigid veins. Passers-by slowed for a moment to look, but then moved on – 'Not my problem,' they thought.

A society is measured not by how many flashy new shopping centres it has, or by how many expensive Audi cars are being driven around in the streets. It is measured by how its people treat and respond to each other in times of need, and that applies to *any* country. I flagged down a police car, leaving them to dig out the unfortunate snow-covered man, before continuing on my way.

Back at my apartment, looking at my packed bags and waiting for my taxi driver to buzz his arrival, I noticed a Russian man on the opposite balcony to mine putting out a bird feeder and filling it with nuts. When it was full, he hung it up on the edge of his icy balcony, before going back inside his apartment, his boots leaving imprints in the fluffy snow. Grateful little sparrows immediately flew over from frozen tree branches to peck and gnaw at the nuts. In any community, it's the giving without wanting or demanding financial recompense that binds its people together; having empathy for your fellow humans and other sentient beings who share the planet with us. A snowy blizzard began to sweep across the view as my door buzzer rang like an alarm clock, waking me from my reverie.

My time was up.

EPILOGUE

'Pussy Riot were doing what punk bands do'

Sometime later, I returned to Moscow for one last short visit. I still had three big suitcases of clothes and things which I had not been able to take with me on my departure (I was amazed at how much stuff I'd amassed during my time in Russia) and which I'd left with my friend Elizaveta. When I arrived, I decided to take her out to the cinema and for a meal, as a 'thank you' for looking after my stuff. The Russian cinematic experience is somewhat different to what you and I are accustomed to. For one thing, people don't turn off their phones, and have absolutely no qualms about taking calls and talking loudly. Most Western films are dubbed into Russian, with no subtitles. Most Russians want to see their characters talking and don't like having to read stuff at the bottom of the screen. So accordingly, each actor had a dedicated dubbing artist assigned to do their voice, which never changed. That was because the audience became accustomed to hearing a particular voice for a particular actor. After all, imagine if you went to see a Samuel L. Jackson film, and then the following week you saw him in another film and his voice sounded different – it would be weird, right? Therefore, each Russian dubbing artist held on to the same Western actor for life. Great if 'your' actor is appearing in loads of films, but if he or she died or just had a bad year, then you would have a bad year too. Anyway, a couple of cinemas would show one film a week in its original format, presumably for Russians who wanted to practise their English. So we ended up seeing *Tron: Legacy*, a Disney science-fiction special effects-laden sequel, a copy of which had somehow managed to evade being exported back to America, and was still being shown in an obscure and ornately decorated Russian cinema. The film, however, in my opinion, was a stinker. Here was a plot that was supposed to be about how the human soul can overcome the constraints of technology, yet it was so overblown with special effects that the humanity of the story was completely lost. It had a superb soundtrack, though, done by the group Daft Punk. So just listening to that sweeping music in a proper auditorium was a lovely two-hour experience. In some ways, the flick was an allegory for Moscow, in a structural sense – all brash and impressive-looking, but not always much substance underneath it all. Russians do chortle in odd places in films. Any reference to Russia is usually met with howls of laughter, especially when

Western actors put on terrible Russian accents, which is most of the time.

Out on the streets of Moscow, nothing much seemed to have changed. Mr. Putin was still in charge, and a few more glitzy upmarket shopping centres were being built (presumably for oligarchs and their girlfriends to use) to make Moscow look as spruced-up as possible for the 2018 football World Cup.

There is much talk of an emerging 'middle class' in Russia, who might eventually break the mould of mass underprivilege. I for one, though, am not convinced. In the UK, we understand 'middle class' to be people who care about the communal areas in an apartment block, who protest to their local council if the bins are not collected, who engage to some extent with the police – the sort of folk who would stop and help an injured roadside animal, and so forth. Of course, any 'class' can do these things, but in Russia, middle class means rushing into any one of the new Swedish furniture stores so you can renovate your apartment and rent it out with the intent of making a good deal of money from a foreigner. And that's about as far as the community spirit goes. It's just not the same thing, and the majority are not, despite what you might see and read in the media, remotely interested in unbalancing the political status quo. That only comes if the rouble collapses and their savings become worthless – *then* all hell would break loose. And in any case, at the end of the day, who are we to say that Russia should be this or that? Surely, they can make up their own minds, as mercurial as they are.

Meanwhile, the all-female Russian punk band Pussy

Riot were doing what punk bands do, by raising hell and getting into trouble with the authorities. Some said it was a sign of change; that some protest was being allowed, spurred on by the largely ungovernable internet. Not sure if the band members who were sent to jail would agree though. I should at this point apologise to any Russian woman reading this who may feel that I have shown them in a bad light, by tainting them with the broad brush of Russian bride clichés. It was not my intention. I was, after all, on a determined quest to find my other half, and in doing so ended up dating a lot of women. Indeed, my friend Peter ended up marrying a Russian girl. She is intelligent, thoughtful and morally sound. Does she like presents? Well, of course she does. When he goes away on a trip, he makes sure he brings back something for her. In her eyes, it means that at least for part of his trip away, he was thinking of her. And what's wrong with that? Isn't that what romance is supposed to be about? At petrol stations, I had noticed that if a lone female attempted to put diesel into her car unaided, any passing Russian man would invariably step in to do it for her. She would not regard this as unwelcome. On the contrary, in her eyes it meant she would not have to risk getting her dress dirty with oil stains. And what would the stray man demand in recompense? Absolutely nothing. For him, it's just what men do. Sexist and archaic? Or chivalrous and gentlemanly? You decide. As for the Russians as a whole, and their culture and place in the world; well, think of any black-and-white film you've ever seen. Despite the term 'black and white', most of it is actually shades of grey. And the same applies to people, politics and places. With the acquisition of more knowledge and first-hand experience, previously held distinctions and certainties can become blurred, but that blurring is not often explored in this world of relentless social media, where discourse, thought and patience are regarded as fusty old terms, not worthy of instant 'likes' or 'retweets'. Only the easily distinguishable and extreme picture seems to hold sway. I hope my reminiscences have been sufficiently enlightening to stimulate the grey matter in other people's heads, and perhaps lead them to a more thoughtful middle ground, when it comes to views of the Russian populace as a whole. But enough philosophy.

It was time to go. I said goodbye to Elizaveta and took a cab to the airport. It was no longer possible to just flag down any old car, as the government had declared this practice illegal. Now, you had to use 'official' taxis, which was supposed to provide some kind of regulation and safety, though in reality the law had probably been designed to clamp down on people from the Caucasus who were making a small living from unofficial taxi driving. As ever, the poorest and most defenceless in society get the blame for everything.

Would it be true to say that I would miss Moscow? For certain, it is an exciting, but also foreboding city that affects different people in different ways, and as I crunched my boots on the snowy airport tarmac for the last time and made my way up the stairs to the plane, I imagined there would be no turning back (or would there?).

I have since spoken by phone to another couple I had befriended during my time in Moscow. A young British teacher called James and his Russian girlfriend Olga, an accountant. They had been watching a television news report about the British voters' decision to leave the European Union, after the referendum results had been announced. James related their conversation to me.

'I don't understand this Brexit situation,' said Olga.

'What don't you understand?' replied James.

'Well, why did it happen?' she asked, frowning.

'Fifty-two per cent of people voted Leave, while forty-eight per cent voted Remain. So, the Leave voters won.'

'But I still don't get it.'

James looked at her, wondering what she meant.

'What don't you get?'

'Well, it's going to cause the government a lot of problems, right?'

'Probably, yes.'

'Well,' she reasoned with genuine incredulity, 'why didn't the government just stuff some more Remain votes in the boxes? It would have saved them a lot of trouble.'

I couldn't help smiling to myself. A pragmatic Russian solution. Not democracy as we know it, but a holistic approach that some would say has its practical merits, while others would strongly argue is the backbone of dictatorship. Exactly the kind of moral and sociological dilemma that had so challenged my understanding of the world and relationships during my stay in Russia, and had ultimately led to my departure.

I wondered if Deidre, the sexy, barefooted American expat I had met, had also made her escape. Well, my recent British acquaintance never came to anything Deidre, so I'm still up for a date if you are...

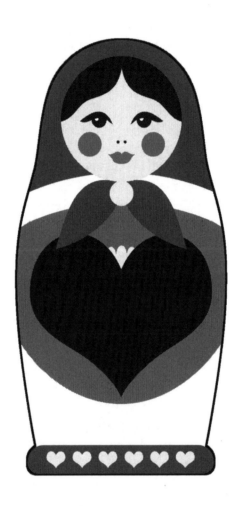